The Parent's Complete Guide to Soccer

The Parent's Complete Guide to Soccer

JOE PROVEY

Foreword by U.S. Soccer Gold Medalist
MICHELLE AKERS

The Lyons Press
Guilford, Connecticut
An imprint of The Globe Pequot Press

To buy books in quantity for corporate use
or incentives, call **(800) 962–0973, ext. 4551,**
or e-mail **premiums@GlobePequot.com.**

The Lyons Press is an imprint of The Globe Pequot Press.

10   9   8   7   6   5   4   3 , 2   1

Printed in the United States of America

Illustrations by Andrew Vallas

Library of Congress Cataloging-in-Publication Data

Provey, Joe.
  The parent's complete guide to soccer / Joe Provey ; foreword by Michelle Akers. -- 1st ed.
     p. cm.
  Includes index.
  ISBN 1-59228-852-9 (trade paper)
  1. Soccer for children--Training. 2. Soccer for children--Coaching. I. Title.
GV943.9.T7P76 2005
796.334'083--dc22

                                    2005021541

To Tom Mindrum and Horst Weber,
my Soccer JR. *partners and good friends.*

Contents

Foreword

I first began playing soccer at the age of eight on a team in Santa Clara, California, called the Cougars. Our uniforms were pink and yellow (my second worst nightmare), and we lost every single game we played (my worst nightmare). And, as it happens in most youth soccer teams around the United States, a couple of well-meaning, enthusiastic, committed moms (my mom being one of them), who were totally clueless when it came to the game of soccer, were our first coaches. Not that their lack of soccer knowledge was the reason we lost every single game (though I think the pink and yellow uniforms played a part in that), but it sure didn't help that they had no idea what the rules of the game were, what positions to put us in and the responsibility of each, how to teach skills and put together a practice, or what doggone colors to pick for our uniforms.

This book by Joe Provey would have been a lifeboat and a godsend to not only our soccer-clueless moms, but to us as well. Who knows, maybe if this book had been around when I was a little girl, we still might have looked like dorks in our pink and yellow uniforms, but at least we might have won a few games to even things out. I am positive this book will be invaluable to all parents who are new to the game and want not only to become educated about the basics of soccer and what to expect during a soccer season, but to help their kids have the best soccer experience of their lives.

Michelle Akers
Olympic and World Cup Champion

Acknowledgments

We wish to thank the following people for generously sharing their soccer and parenting knowledge: Michelle Akers, Ed Borg, Andy Caruso, Dean Conway, Efrain "Chico" Chacurian, Tony DiCicco, Bob Dikranian, Larry Sashin, Jill Schoff, Charla Scofield, Henrik Svartborn, and Priscilla Williams.

Introduction

In the glorious days of early parenthood when my two boys, Joseph and Renald, were ages four and one respectively, my wife, Deborah, and I were living in Minneapolis. We had moved there from Connecticut for my new job—editing a do-it-yourself home improvement magazine. In the long-lit spring evenings, we'd take drives to explore our new city. Often we'd drive by athletic fields with "big" boys and girls running in every direction, chasing a ball. I can still see the scene in that low, slanting light that intensifies every color and throws long purple shadows. Kids in blue or red or yellow uniforms. Parents standing on the sidelines, the cheers just reaching our open car windows as we drove by.

I told the boys that the game was soccer and that one day I would teach them to play. I told them that I'd played it back in the Connecticut town where I grew up—and that we were the high school state champions in 1966! I told them that it was a great sport, harder but more fun than any of the others I had tried.

Seeing the kids playing made me wonder where the teams had come from. What organization had sponsored the play? How did one register a child for a team and at what age? Was it something peculiar to the Midwest? My own soccer experience was almost entirely through the public school system, first as an intramural program in junior high school and then as a varsity sport in high school. But the games we saw being played in the parks of Minneapolis did not appear to be part of any school program.

It all remained a mystery until a few years later when we landed back in Connecticut. I had taken a new job editing another how-to magazine and was commuting to New York City from the suburbs. One fall day Joseph, now a first-grader, brought home a notice from school about a town-sponsored youth soccer league. I checked the box that asked if I was interested in helping out. About a week later, I got a call asking if I would help coach a team. Sure, I said—even though it had been years since I had played.

There was little in those first few years of coaching to tell me how soccer would become such a huge part of my life. Our team, the Eagles, practiced one hour a week and played a match every Saturday morning in the spring and fall. I yelled myself hoarse every weekend, along with all the rest of the coaches, exhorting our boys to battle. We were so backward and ignorant as youth coaches that when it was left up to us, we played with an unmanageable nine and even ten six-year-olds on a side—far too many, as we would learn later. We encouraged our charges to play an athletic brand of bump-and-run soccer—and we were absurdly proud of all the wins we racked up.

Eventually, our local soccer club president suggested that all coaches get coaching licenses. We did and gradually began to see the light. Some fathers started to get together on Sundays for pickup games on their own. We were joined by expatriates and immigrants from many countries—places where kids grow up with the sport. Eventually it dawned on us that there was a lot more to soccer than we had ever imagined.

By 1991, I was coaching both of my sons' teams and was looking forward to coaching my daughter Corinna's first-grade recreation team. (And working at yet another home how-to magazine—this time, thankfully, with offices near my home in Connecticut.) I was a league director, on the board of the local soccer club, and playing twice a week myself. Soccer had become a year-round, many-hour commitment. It was then that I learned that the magazine I was working for was being sold to a publisher on the West Coast.

Neither the magazine's art director, my friend Horst Weber, nor I wanted to move. After several lunches discussing subjects for magazines we would like to launch ourselves, we settled upon soccer. About this time, Joseph complained that Time Inc.'s *Sports Illustrated for Kids* ran few soccer articles. His comment helped us decide that our new publication should be a soccer magazine for kids. When fellow soccer dad and entrepreneur Tom Mindrum heard our idea—between matches at a youth soccer tournament (where else?)—he decided to build a small publishing company around it.

We published *Soccer JR.* for the next ten years. At one time it was the biggest paid-circulation soccer magazine in the United States, boasting 150,000 subscribers and a million readers. The publishing business, as anyone who has tried it knows, is a difficult one. In 2002, due to a downturn in advertising by companies like Nike and Adidas, we were forced to sell it to Scholastic Corp., a big book and magazine marketer and publisher that managed to lose sight of *Soccer JR.*'s mission: to deliver a quality magazine to youth soccer players of America. Scholastic eventually ceased publication of the magazine in 2003. Tom, Horst, and the rest of the *Soccer JR.* staff, however, rest easy—knowing that many of our millions of readers have gone on to play at high levels in college and the pros. Many more continue to enjoy the sport in adult amateur leagues. We're also sure that some other soccer-crazy lovers of the sport will try to succeed some day where we failed.

CHAPTER 1

Why Soccer?

There are many good reasons why over 11 million children play soccer in the United States. It's fun. You only need a ball, a little space, and a few friends to play. It challenges kids to become fit, learn skills, communicate, work together, and be creative. Soccer is a sport in which kids can make their own decisions and have equal opportunities to shine. Players do not have to be big or tall or have great hand-eye coordination.

Drive by the athletic fields in nearly any suburban town (or urban park, for that matter) and you'll see kids playing soccer. And it's not just young children. In the past fifteen years (1989 to 2004), high school soccer participation has grown over 100 percent, faster than any other major sport, according to the National Federation of State High School Associations.

Youth soccer dominates team sports in the United States. In the last twenty years it has surpassed baseball, football, hockey, and basketball as the team sport of choice. Lacrosse and roller hockey, although growing in popularity, are still just blips on the radar screen of youth sports by comparison.

Number-One Sport on the Planet

The rest of the world was bitten by the soccer bug long ago (called football in most places). There are more than 250 million registered players worldwide—and that's just a small fraction of total players. There are also more member countries (205) in FIFA (Fédération Internationale de Football Association), soccer's governing body, than there are in the United Nations. Countries as small as Vietnam have professional soccer leagues. The Cape Verde Islands take the sport as seriously as Brazil does. And the World Cup, which rolls around every four years, is a bigger event than the World Series, Super Bowl, and NBA Finals combined. It's a two-year process to merely qualify for the final round, which is a monthlong event. The 2002 World Cup was watched by an estimated worldwide TV audience (discrete viewings) of 28.8 billion, including 1.1 billion for the final game.

Internationally, soccer has the power to bring all kinds of people together, promoting the exchange of ideas and mutual understanding. Every nation has its own style of play and its own soccer culture. Soccer even brings unfriendly nations together. At World Cup '98 in France, U.S. and Iranian players put their respective nations' political hostility aside and posed for pictures, shook hands, and exchanged jerseys—a sign of respect among players.

An Edge over Traditional Youth Sports

Soccer is popular among kids because in every match, at any moment, every player has the opportunity to do something important. Although the best-skilled and most athletic players "touch" or handle the ball more than others, everyone has a role and is involved. In soccer, kids don't get banished to the outfield because they can't field and the coach hopes the ball will never be hit there.

This not only makes soccer an equal-opportunity sport, but also one of the most physically demanding. Kids are almost always running, leaping, and kicking when playing soccer. Surveys indicate that one of the main reasons kids play sports is to stay fit. Few sports produce athletes that can rival soccer players for overall fitness. It is not uncommon to hear stories about high school athletes who are able to walk off a soccer field and onto a cross-country, field hockey, track, volleyball, lacrosse, or football team and immediately become stars thanks to their superior fitness. In fact, high school coaches of other sports often complain that the best athletes have chosen soccer, leaving their teams depleted.

Another big advantage to soccer is the thinking part of the game. It has been compared to chess, but with twenty-two minds—not just two—trying to find the best moves. In soccer much of the decision-making responsibility rests with the players—not the coach. Unlike football, basketball, hockey, and baseball, there is very little coaching done during a match. The clock only stops at halftime, and there are no timeouts. This makes soccer a play-ers' game, not one that's dominated by coaches' signals or plays called in from the bench. A youth coach pre-pares the team during training ses-sions and then should sit back and try to enjoy the match.

Because players call the shots, soccer is an excellent training ground for leaders. Kids who are natural leaders can develop their skills—un-less, of course, a misguided coach becomes too involved.

Soccer is also a great way for children to learn about teamwork because it is a sport that gets every-one involved. Players must continu-ally work together to find ways to meet challenges and to score goals. Kids quickly learn that the team can only be successful if ways are found for every player to contribute.

Soccer is challenging to kids be-cause it demands that every player, regardless of the position played, master a range of skills. It's a little like scouting, with its merit badges. The harder you work, the higher the level you can achieve. Passing, chipping, volleying, shooting, jug-gling, swerving, driving, heading, throwing, receiving—the list is exten-sive. Mastering these skills involves tremendous dedication.

Finally, compared to many other youth sports, soccer has fewer serious injuries. There is no one throwing a hardball in your direction. No one is trying to knock you to the ground or hit you with a stick. This is not to say there are no injuries in soccer. There's plenty of body-to-body contact, and minor injuries are common, especially to the legs and feet. Injuries to the head have also become a concern, primarily with older youth players, and will be addressed in later chapters.

Great for Boys and Girls

Soccer is a great sport for boys and girls. Although traditionally the sport has attracted more boys than girls, the gap is narrowing. In 2004, nearly half of all high school players in the United States were female.

Most girls seem to prefer to play on all-girl teams. Research in the early '80s showed that participation of girls in youth soccer leagues rocketed whenever a league changed its policy from forming coed teams to putting girls and boys on separate teams.

The differences between the play of girls and boys, up until puberty, are not great. Young girls have the edge when it comes to understanding teamwork. They quickly grasp the benefits of passing. Boys seem to focus a little more on getting the ball and scoring goals. They like to shoot; left to their own devices, they do not like to pass the ball.

These are, of course, generalizations. There are exceptions in both groups—girls who make a beeline straight to the goal each time they get the ball, and boys who are content to send through passes to their teammates from the midfield all day long.

Viewpoint: Soccer Is Different

Our weekly adult pickup soccer match takes place at a multisport complex of fields. One evening, as we stretched our old muscles in preparation for the late summer game, a Pop Warner football practice session with perhaps a dozen teams of various ages was in progress on a field next to us. On a field in the other direction, a Babe Ruth League baseball match was in progress. Across the street, there was a party of golfers making their way through the local par-3 golf course.

On the football field, about a dozen enormous men were talking loudly to miniature players who huddled about them in circles across the field. Occasionally, the huddle would break apart and the players would bump their helmets or shoulder pads against each other or fall to the ground and roll over a few times. Then it was back to the huddle. Meanwhile, on the diamond, fifteen players stood motionless, two were playing catch, and one was poised with a bat, watching the pitches go by. Another dozen players sat on benches. There was so little movement, it looked like a painting. Once every few minutes, someone would hit a ball. There would be a little activity—rarely more than two dozen steps in any direction—and then everyone would return to their original positions. Need I go into detail about what was happening on the golf course?

Ten minutes later, our match began. The soccer pitch was filled with players jogging or sprinting, first in one direction, then the other. Not everyone was near the ball. If there was an empty area on the field, players ran to fill it and to call for a pass. Even the goalkeeper was in nearly constant motion, moving forward with his team on attack, retreating when under pressure, throwing, and punting.

When I coached young girls, I occasionally had the opportunity to have my team scrimmage against boys of similar age. I noticed that the girls easily held their own through elementary school and early middle school. When playing boys, the girls seemed to play harder than they did when playing girls. The rallying cry "Play like you're playing boys!" became our team's inside joke and was invoked whenever the girls seemed listless and unfocused. Upon hearing it, most of the team would become energized and very assertive—much to the surprise of their opponents.

Should a Girl Play on a Boys' Team?

Many girls who have played on boys' teams say it's great—if you have the ability and desire. They claim that the experience of playing on a boys' team forced them to be quicker and more physically assertive. This is a preparation that many elite girl players have chosen, including many players on the women's national team.

In my limited experience, I have seen girls on boys' teams who matched up well against boy opponents up until the age of fourteen or fifteen, as well as girls on boys' teams who were limited to the role of occasional sub. In the latter case, I believe that more playing time on an all-girl team will outweigh any benefits that come from training with boys.

Coed scrimmages, however, are another story. One U-14 boys' team I coached loved to scrimmage the U-15 girls' team that shared our field after practice. The feeling was mutual for obvious—and not so obvious—reasons. The soccer that was played was just as much a focal point as the socializing.

These matches were the highlights of the boys' and girls' afternoons, and parents were often kept waiting while the kids played well past the official end time of the practice. Any sort of imbalance in the strength of the teams could be easily remedied by swapping one or two players.

Size Doesn't Matter

Unlike basketball and football, size is not necessarily a factor in soccer. Good players come in all sizes and shapes. The average height in Major League Soccer is about 5 foot 11. Pelé, who is acknowledged to be the greatest player of all time, was 5 foot 7. Diego Maradona, the Argentine star who dominated soccer through much of the '80s and '90s, is only 5 foot 4. Cobi Jones, the sparkplug of the Los Angeles Galaxy, weighs in at 140 pounds. Roselli, the star forward of the Brazilian women's national team, is 5 foot 1. Mia Hamm weighs 125 pounds. The list could easily go on to fill up this page.

Some coaches claim there's an advantage to being small. Small youth players are forced to develop skills and use their wits sooner than big players, who can rely on strength and speed. As a result, they begin to play the game at a sophisticated level at an earlier age. Big, strong kids who get by on their athleticism during their early years but who have weak skills sometimes get left behind once they reach high school and college. By then, everyone has reached puberty and the playing field levels.

This is not to say that athleticism doesn't matter. It does—especially speed. A modestly skilled player with exceptional speed will almost

Viewpoint: Playing Up Can Be a Downer?

Last fall I received an e-mail from "Jim," a soccer dad and reader of the *Soccer for Parents* magazine we publish. "Jane," his nine-year-old daughter, was playing up on a U-11 select team and was not getting much playing time. Her skills were fine, but most of the other girls were a full year older—and stronger. Although Jim thought the coach was great and that Jane was getting plenty of training (six hours a week), he felt that his daughter was on the wrong team. Unfortunately, Jane didn't see it that way and did not want to drop down to a team at her own age level. She didn't want to leave her friends, and she felt proud to be a member of the team. What to do?

I responded by saying that I don't believe that any nine-year-old should be playing on a select team, let alone playing up on a select team. I also mentioned that six hours of training per week for nine- and ten-year-olds was too much. My feeling is that kids play on competitive teams at too early an age. The reason for this is complex. It typically has to do with the way youth soccer is organized (like a ladder), combined with parents' natural desire not to see their child fall behind or be unhappy. To be sure, some very determined parents push their kids into competitive situations in hope of ensuring a spot on the high school team or on a college team, but my sense is that they are in the minority.

Of course, this wasn't much help to Jane and her parents. She was already on the team. I went on to say that there were two choices: Gently explain to Jane that she would have more fun and would improve more quickly on a team that would always help win more games than will a highly skilled player who is slow. Is this fair? No. But it's reality. Many American coaches who are already predisposed to favor size, strength, and speed from coaching traditional sports will cut the skillful player and roster the exceptional athlete.

A coach's preferred style of play is also a factor in whether size is important or not. If a coach has built a game around strength and power and your child looks like the "before" portrait in an ad for nutritional supplements, expect him to become very familiar with the bench. Taller kids will get the nod if the coach's favorite tactic is to play long balls into the box instead of building to a finish with short, controlled passes. Of course, if your child is on the small side, you can always look for a team coached by someone who prefers a possession style of play.

give her more playing time. Or, let her continue with her current team and risk her eventually becoming discouraged and quitting the sport altogether. In my opinion, short-term disappointment was better than turning Jane away from a lifetime sport she apparently loves.

Recently I contacted Jane's parents to see what they had decided to do. Her father reported that in the spring Jane had tried out both for her team and for an age-correct team. She made both squads but wanted to stay with the older group— which her parents allowed her to do, even though she is the last player off the bench. The fact that Jane's team dropped from playing at the A level to the C level was also a factor in deciding to allow Jane to continue playing up. Jim reports that she enjoys cheering from the sideline and doesn't complain about her limited playing time.

Jane's parents believe the decision to play up should be left to the child— unless the higher level poses an excessive risk of physical injury. They hope that when Jane starts playing on her middle school team, she will develop friendships with players her own age and be more willing to change teams.

Did they make a good decision?

It's too early to tell. It sounds as though they know their daughter well and are making the best of a difficult situation. The moral of the story, of course, is to be very careful about moving an unprepared child into a competitive playing situation. "Because all of my friends are doing it" isn't always a good enough reason.

As a child gets older, some coaches feel that size may affect the choice of position to concentrate upon. Generally speaking, taller players have some advantages on defense with their ability to clear away dangerous incoming crosses with their heads. Tall goalkeepers also have an edge because they can cover more of the goal opening. Smaller players, with their ability to make quick moves in small spaces, often dominate the midfield. Up front it's good to have a mix of tall and short players, the former a target for long services into the goal area and the latter valued for their ability to move and shoot quickly.

Dangers of Playing Up

As a parent, it's wise to avoid situations where your child is at a severe disadvantage because of size, speed, and athleticism. If the opportunity arises for your child to play up (play on a team in an older age group), think twice. Playing with bigger, more mature players may result in injuries. In one such case, a ten-year-old girl playing two years up, on a U-13 team, had her leg broken in several places in a collision with the goalkeeper. She now has a steel rod in her leg and may never play again. Unfortunately, it is a common practice for preteen girls to play with older and bigger teenagers in towns where there are not enough girls to fill out rosters of age-specific teams.

Concerns about Heading

Heading—the practice of striking the ball with the head to shoot, pass, or clear a ball—has become a controversial issue in the last few years. Several studies have compared adult professional soccer players to other groups in the general population, such as swimmers and track athletes, who do not typically engage in activities similar to heading. The results indicate that the soccer players have signs of neurological damage, as evidenced by their scores on various tests, including verbal memory, visual memory, and planning. It is uncertain whether these tests have any relevance to heading by youth players, but they are cause for concern.

Most of the reports hypothesize two possible dangers from heading: routine head-to-ball contact in matches and training sessions, and concussions that result from heading activity. Most experts suggest that risks due to routine heading are minimal or nonexistent as long as heading is done in moderation and using proper technique (see chapter 5).

Concussions are the more serious problem. They typically occur when two or more players try to head the ball at the same time and collide head to head. Concussions can also be caused by collisions with elbows, knees, the ground, or goalposts. On rare occasions, concussions may also be caused by being unexpectedly hit in the head with a kicked ball.

To make matters worse, young kids whose skulls are not mature are more susceptible to damage from concussions than are older players. In addition, many concussions go unrecognized or are forgotten. This is dangerous because damage from concussions is cumulative. The more concussions a player suffers, the greater the risk of problems later. The worst-case scenario is successive concussions within a short period of time. Successive concussions can cause severe brain damage or even death.

Heading is not a big issue until kids begin to use the skill at age ten or eleven. Once they do, there is much that coaches can do to minimize risk from heading (see "Heading" in chapter 5 and "Teaching Heading" in chapter 10).

CHAPTER 2

Getting Started

Some people believe that instilling a love for soccer should begin as soon as a toddler can kick a ball and run after it. Some believe it can begin sooner! But with children under five years old, do not expect or demand too much. Under no circumstances do you want to frustrate your child. You may model the correct ways to dribble, pass, or shoot, but don't try to make your child imitate how you do it. The child's mind doesn't work that way yet. Very young children are simply looking to show the world how wonderful they are. They get pleasure from catching up to the rolling ball and then sending it on its way again. All of this is like a miracle to them. And when they tire of this miracle and get ready to move on to another—such as splashing stones in a puddle—don't try to stop them. Go with the flow. Impose no rules. Your sessions together with the ball may only last a few minutes, but that's OK.

Backyard Fun

As your kids approach school age, begin to play soccerlike games in the backyard. This may be a good time to introduce the no-hands rule, but few others are needed.

While my kids were growing up, we invented a game we called "kick the cone." Many evenings before dinner we would simply place a training cone (available at any soccer or sports store) or plastic bucket in a grassy area with at least ten yards of clear space in all directions. One player guards the cone while the other one (or two) tries to hit the

Figure 2.1: "Kick the Cone" game.

cone with the ball. Once the cone is hit, change roles. If playing with three, rotate.

There are many variations to this game. For instance, you may put a time limit on possession and keep score by seeing who can score the most times in three, five, or seven minutes. Or, in the one-versus-one version of the game, the player in possession of the ball is always the attacker, and the person without the ball is always the defender. As kids get older, you may decide (with them) that a rule is needed to prevent "goal tending." The player winning possession, for example, might have to dribble the ball at least 5 yards away from the cone before being able to attack. Or you may use two cones.

A soccer version of monkey-in-the-middle is also great preparation for young children. Mark two lines with cones about 10 to 15 yards apart. Players 1 and 2 stand outside each line, and the "monkey" stands between them. The object is for players 1 and 2 to complete passes through the monkey's zone. If a pass is intercepted, the player making the pass must move to the middle.

This game also has many variations. You may limit the time a player has to pass (for example, to "three Mississippi") or lengthen the distance between the lines as the players' passing skills improve. You may also add more kids to either end or to the middle and experiment with adding balls. In this version, award one point for each completed pass and one point for each intercepted pass. (A pass is not complete if it is kicked beyond the receiver.) Rotate roles as desired.

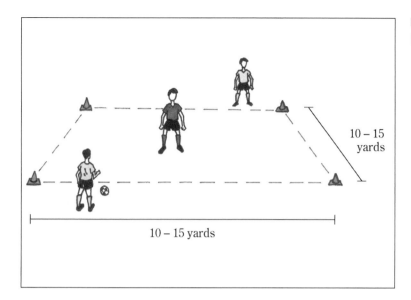

Figure 2.2: "Monkey-in-the-Middle" game.

Games can be a lot simpler, too. Simply dribbling a wadded-up ball of paper around a room can be fun. (If you want to get fancy, stuff the paper ball into an old sock or stocking, twist behind the wad, reinsert the ball portion into the remaining tube, and repeat until no excess fabric is left.)

Larry Sashin, a longtime soccer innovator and coach, began teaching skills to his kids with tennis balls. "I'd stand about ten feet away and lay a plastic garbage can at my side. The object was to control the ball and try to kick it into the garbage can."

He also played soccer golf in his house with paper balls. The doorways were the "holes," and the players' feet were the clubs. As the kids became more skilled, he shrank the doorway openings with shoes and slippers. Outdoors, he played the same game, but with trees and stones as holes.

To play soccer bowling, you only need a set of plastic pins. Set them up in a hall (or yard) and have kids shoot at them with a small ball. Vary the distance and angle according to the players' ability.

For large groups of players of varying ages and skill levels, soccer baseball is fun. In soccer baseball, batters kick the ball to an open space or as far as they can. If the opposing team can return the ball to home plate before the runner rounds all of the bases, they get an out. If not, a "run" scores. If playing with a mix of younger and older kids, make a rule that the young kids only need to touch one or two bases before heading for home plate. Play with or without a "pitcher" and

change sides when a team has made three outs or batted around the order.

The rules of other common games can be modified to apply to soccer, but not all are suitable for very young children. For example, soccer volleyball (played over a picnic table or low net) restricts players from using their hands. Otherwise, the rules for volleyball apply. Kids usually must reach ten or eleven before they can successfully play soccer volleyball.

Whenever you come up with a game, remember to give older kids a handicap. That way everyone has a chance to win and feel successful.

Playing "Real" Soccer

Small-sided backyard soccer games during family get-togethers or with neighborhood children are the best way to learn the game. Three or four children per side are ideal, but it's OK to have more. Adapt the rules to your space and to the ages of the children. If the older kids are dominating, suggest they only pass and shoot with their weak foot. Play without keepers if you choose. Instead, make the goals small or make a rule that shots must roll in on the ground or below knee level. Eliminate corner kicks and goal kicks on small fields; simply allow the defending team to put the ball back into play from its endline. Encourage the kids to make their own rules. It's important to help kids discover simple ways to play soccer on their own for when you're not around.

Gearing Up with Goals, Rebounders, and Kick Walls

Before investing a lot of money in backyard equipment, consider using the common items you may already have on hand. A sturdy wooden picnic table laid on its side may make a good kick wall for a six- or seven-year-old. Picnic table benches make good goals for small-sided backyard matches. The limb of a tree can support a soccer pendulum (foam ball attached to a cord) for improving timing when heading a ball. Fences or garage walls skinned over with half-inch plywood can serve as a kick wall for older children.

As your child gets older, consider adding a rebounder (see chapter 8). These products typically consist of a metal frame with netting

Figure 2.3:
"Rebounder" game. Teams score by shooting at either side of the net.

stretched across the face of the frame. When a ball is kicked, thrown, or headed against it, the net returns the ball to the child. Rebounder nets may also be stretched across a garage door opening. They are commercially available and cut to standard-size garage door openings.

Rebounders serve nicely as goals, but many fun games can be played with them as well. A favorite at my house is played by placing the rebounder in the center of an area at least 20 by 20 yards. Each side of the rebounder is a goal. A player (or a team of players) scores by hitting either side of the net. It's a simple game that teaches many soccer skills: dribbling, shooting, passing and receiving (when playing with more than one versus one), and even chipping and heading when the kids reach nine or ten years old.

Backyard goals are also worth considering, especially if you have a large play area and many children interested in soccer in your neighborhood. Although it's more satisfying for kids to score in a goal that looks like a real goal, the rebounder mentioned earlier is more versatile—and kids don't have to stop playing to retrieve their balls. In addition, rebounders are easier than goals to move and store.

Preschool Soccer Programs

There are many soccer programs available for preschoolers and kindergartners, often administered by YMCAs, PALs, Boys and Girls Clubs, indoor soccer centers, church organizations, or town recreation

Building a Kick Wall

If you're handy and have room in your yard, it's not difficult to build a small kick wall. Set two 4 x 4 posts into the ground, 8 feet apart (measured outside to outside). Use pressure-treated posts to prevent rot. It's wise to set the posts below the frost line in your region. In the north, for instance, that means you should dig holes 3 feet deep. Brace the posts with strips of scrap wood and wooden stakes after using a level to ensure they are plumb (vertical in two directions). Then, backfill with gravel and soil, and tamp (pound with the top of a sledge hammer) until firm; or pour a collar of ready-mix concrete so the wall will be able to take a pounding without budging.

Frame between the posts with 2 x 4s, as you would the wall of a house—a top and bottom plate with studs 16 inches on center. Then fasten a ¾ inch sheet of exterior-grade plywood to each side of the wall. Put the smooth sides facing out. Use screws and be sure to sink the screw heads below the surface of the plywood. Prime and paint the wall. Get creative by painting marks on the wall to serve as targets.

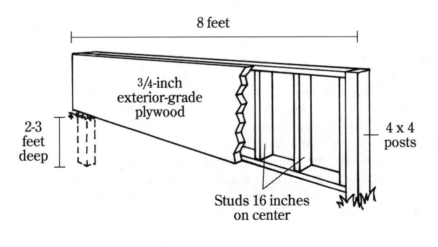

8 feet

3/4-inch exterior-grade plywood

2-3 feet deep

4 x 4 posts

Studs 16 inches on center

departments. Although these programs are well-intentioned, be cautious if you are considering enrolling your child. The programs can do more harm than good to children who are not yet ready for group play.

David Carr, a national coaching director for U.S. Soccer, conducted research on the subject at Ohio University. He suggests that playing organized soccer at too early an age generates emotional stress and can cause kids to drop out before giving the sport a chance. I've seen this happen—and the child in question never played soccer again. Carr advises parents to avoid toddler programs where children play games that resemble real soccer and where scores are kept.

Carr notes that many young children have bodies that are top-heavy. They enjoy chasing the ball and kicking it, but most will become frustrated when told to try even simple skills such as passing with the inside of the foot, receiving the ball with the arch of the foot, and shooting with the instep. Carr says that most children at this age are reactionary in their movements. Children have trouble anticipating where a ball will be kicked next and in controlling balls that are bouncing or coming to them in the air. Nor can they listen to and understand involved instructions. My good friend's son, Eric, a bright five-year-old, could not master the idea of using the inside of the foot for passing—despite patient instruction from his father and me.

Playing in groups is uncommon for children under five years old. The world is still very egocentric for children this age. Even many kindergartners are not ready developmentally to play on a team, says Carr. Any sort of criticism or perceived failure becomes enormous in the mind of the child—and can lead to a frustrating experience for parent and child, one that may sour the child's feeling about soccer forever.

In my own experience, young kids (under seven) have no real interest in who is winning or what the score is. They only become interested if they see it is of concern to their moms, dads, and coaches. Children at this age are very sensitive and will often burst into tears if criticized. Even gentle criticism will often be rejected. If you do decide to sign your child up for a "tot" program, try to find one that is solely for fun with noncompetitive activities that promote coordination and familiarity with the ball.

Finally, keep in mind there is no rush to move your child into organized soccer. The great Argentine star Gabriel Batistuta did not begin playing soccer until he was sixteen! Today he is six goals shy of setting the record for most goals scored in World Cup play.

How to Know When Your Child Is Ready to Join a Team

Children develop according to their own schedules, not necessarily according to their birthdays. If you're not sure your child is ready for organized soccer, answer the following true or false questions and rate your child's readiness using the scoring outline at the end.

1. My child prefers to play alone rather than with a playmate.   T or F

2. My child is willing to try new ways to do familiar tasks.   T or F

3. My child has problems with taking turns.   T or F

4. I don't usually have to repeat directions to my child.   T or F

5. My child becomes upset when I point out that something
   is being done the wrong way.   T or F

6. My child does not normally mind sharing toys.   T or F

7. My child has not yet developed the coordination and
   physical ability of other children of the same age.   T or F

8. My child has expressed an interest in playing soccer.   T or F

9. My child is uncomfortable around adults other than parents
   and relatives.   T or F

10. My child can concentrate on a task, such as coloring pictures
    or building with blocks, for more than 10 minutes at a time.   T or F

Scoring: If you answered true to most of the odd-numbered statements and false to most of the even-numbered statements, your child is probably not ready for organized soccer. Continue to play soccer in the backyard and invite a few friends or siblings to join in as your child becomes more confident. If you answered in the reverse, proceed to the next chapter!

CHAPTER 3

Joining a Team

When to begin playing organized team soccer is an important decision. Although there is no "right" age, most kids begin between five and eight years old. When and if to move your child from a recreational program to a more competitive travel team is just as critical. In this chapter you may review the various offerings and select the one that's right for your child. Keep in mind that for a young child (ten and under), your decision will likely be based on age. For children who are a little older, it will depend on age, the level of play you desire for your child, and how much time and money you're willing to commit.

Recreation or In-House Soccer Programs

When your child is ready for playing more structured soccer—typically upon reaching first or second grade—make telephone calls to find out what programs or leagues are available in your town. Generally called "recreation" or "in-house" leagues, they may be administered by your town's parks and recreation department, the American Youth Soccer Organization (AYSO), indoor soccer centers, a youth organization such as the YMCA, or the U.S. Youth Soccer Association (USYSA) affiliated soccer club in your town. There may be several program offerings—or your decision may be a no-brainer because there's only one game in town.

Recreation soccer programs are available for children in elementary and middle school, and sometimes for older kids. There are usually no tryouts, at least not for the purpose of putting the best players on

---

Age-Appropriate Introductions to Soccer

1–3 years:	**Ball rolling, ball catching, and chasing games.**
4–5 years:	**Running and kicking games.**
6–8 years:	**Small-sided soccer (3v3 or 4v4 or 6v6) without a goalkeeper and without keeping scores or league standings.**
9–10 years:	**Small-sided soccer (up to 8v8) with a goalkeeper. Keeping score is inevitable but should be downplayed.**
11 and older:	**Full-sided matches, small-sided games during practice. Scores and standings may be kept but should be downplayed.**

---

one or two teams. Everyone who signs up is put on a team with the promise of playing at least half the game. Teams are typically formed on the basis of age and school district—not by talent—although it's common for some children to be mixed with kids from nearby schools in order to fill out rosters that need players.

Recreation teams are coached by volunteers, usually the parent of a team member. Volunteer coaches are selected by a league director, a club's coaching director, or the club's coaching committee. Occasionally a high school player or interested nonparent will volunteer to coach. Cost to register is low. Uniforms are colored T-shirts or two-colored, reversible jerseys. Team sizes vary, ranging from eight to ten for young teams and ten to eighteen for older teams. Game formats are typically "small-sided" (played with between three and eight players on a side; see the chart on page 101). Training sessions are usually held once a week. Play is usually within a town, keeping travel to a minimum.

Recreation teams, especially older teams, may play in tournaments but usually do not. The American Cup is an annual national soccer tournament for players registered with the U.S. Youth Soccer Association. It is expressly for recreation-level teams and is administered by some state soccer associations. Neither teams nor individuals registered to play in a state cup tournament are eligible for the American Cup.

Travel or Select Soccer Programs

Between the ages of nine and twelve, children are often faced with a decision to continue playing recreation soccer or to try to "make" a travel or select team. Membership is open to the children who live in the town or city where the club is located, but sometimes out-of-town players are accepted—especially if there is no program available in the town in which they live. Teams are formed by age, although players are sometimes permitted to play up (play for teams in older age groups) but not down (for younger teams). In the USYSA, for example, a U-9 team is made up of players who have turned nine by the first day of August.

Most travel teams require kids to try out for the team. Tryouts are typically two-session affairs, overseen by coaches and the club's coaching director (if it has one). Unfortunately, tryouts are often inadequate for assessing soccer potential.

Travel teams are formed within local soccer clubs that are affiliated with one of the national youth soccer organizations mentioned earlier. Teams participate in leagues that are usually composed of teams from clubs from surrounding towns. Travel teams usually play in two or three tournaments per season, including one tournament administered by the state association for the purpose of determining a state champion.

Travel teams are usually coached by parent volunteers who are required to have a beginner-level state coaching license, such as an E or F license. Sometimes travel teams hire paid part-time or full-time coaches or trainers. Typically, players try out and are assigned to A-, B-, and C-level teams based on their playing ability.

Unfortunately, many clubs do not offer more than two or three travel teams per age group—and offer even fewer teams as kids reach high school age. The official reasons for the limited number of teams are typically "not enough good players," "too few fields," and "too few coaches." Although these are factors, the unstated reason is often because these clubs (and the parents who run them) are not interested

in fielding teams that will have losing records. Nor are they interested in distributing the talent base equally among many teams, for the same reason. Therefore, the unfortunate practice of "limiting" participation to "better" players continues in youth soccer, as it does in many other youth sports.

The limiting is done by "cutting," the practice of having kids try out for the team—and then selecting the "best" players and telling the rest they are not wanted. Cutting

What's a Soccer Club?

Soccer clubs are town-based organizations made up of local volunteers. They are usually run by a board of directors and take care of important functions such as reserving fields, registering and insuring players, procuring equipment, training and hiring coaches and referees, and raising funds. Typically, clubs form teams in several age groups and sometimes at more than one level of play. The clubs are often affiliated with state or regional organizations, which in turn are part of national organizations such as AYSO, USYSA, or the Soccer Association for Youth (SAY). Clubs are typically assigned to districts based on geography and play within district-based leagues. The leagues are made up of teams from nearby clubs.

players is contrary to why youth sports exist—for kids to have fun. Kids who are cut, especially if they have played a season or two on a travel team, often quit playing—well before anyone can judge whether they will develop into good players or not. My son Renald is a good example of a child whose potential was not apparent. Slow at nine, he blossomed at thirteen and scored goals for the high school varsity as a freshman. More important, kids who are cut are being denied an opportunity to play the sport they love with their friends.

Cutting players is shortsighted in other ways, too. Many travel teams cut players when they don't need them. A few seasons later, however, after having their top players recruited to play for a premier team, they frequently find it difficult to fill out their rosters. The players they cut only a year or two ago are no longer part of the player pool because they have become discouraged and quit.

Elite or Premier Soccer

Elite or premier league soccer is offered for players who upon reaching their teen years—sometimes earlier—are looking for a more competitive soccer experience than travel soccer. Premier teams may be sponsored by a local club or by a club devoted to the premier level of soccer. They are not usually subject to the geographical restrictions that most travel or select teams are subject to. In other words, players who try out for these teams can expect to compete for places on the roster with players from surrounding towns.

Viewpoint: When Kids Must Choose

At *Soccer JR.* magazine, we often got letters and e-mail from unhappy kids who must choose between playing for their old team and playing for a new one. Typically, they have been playing on a recreation team or a "B"-level travel team, but for various reasons must decide whether to play on a more competitive "A" team. The choice is often difficult because playing at the next level usually means leaving old team-mates behind, making a greater time commitment, and facing the prospect of less playing time.

My philosophy is that youth soccer is a form of play. As a result, my advice has always been that fun should take precedence over things like better competition, spiffy uniforms, playing in prestigious tournaments, and preparing for play in high school and college. To me, having fun is even more important than the speed at which a player develops.

Several years ago, when my daughter Corinna played in a USYSA soccer league, she had to decide whether to move from her B-level U-13 team to the club's A team. (Tryouts were being held because, as is often the case, half of the A team had been recruited by an even more competitive premier-level team.) Her decision was difficult because one good friend made the A team and several (tearful) others didn't. To make matters worse, her coach, whom she liked, was staying on as the B team coach. Additionally, she was a dancer, and her lessons and rehearsals took up a lot of time, frequently interfering with soccer practices.

Despite my advice that she stay with the B team, she decided to give the A team a try.

Her decision had little to do with what many defenders of the current youth soccer system claim—that kids want more competitive soccer. It was more about the fear of missing out, of being left behind and tagged as a second-rate player.

Kids shouldn't have to make these kinds of choices at young ages. The system is wrong when it's modeled on the concept of survival of the fittest. This isn't evolution—it's playtime.

Too often, youth soccer tryouts are like musical chairs. When the music stops, there are always a few less chairs than kids. It's time to put our energy into finding ways to include *more* kids, not ways to select the best and exclude the rest.

Corinna's experience on the A team was as I had guessed it would be. She played less, didn't have as much fun as in the past, and had to deal with schedule conflicts all season long. What's more, her game didn't improve significantly.

Premier clubs sometimes have college coaches as coaching directors, offering the promise of an "in" when it comes time for applying to colleges. Teams within these clubs are often coached by paid coaches with high-level national coaching licenses, such as A, B, and C licenses. The team coaches may be college players or college coaches themselves. Program fees can be more than $1,500 per year, and children are expected to make a year-round commitment, including participation in winter indoor leagues and winter practices. Practices may not be held in your town or even in a town nearby, so soccer moms of premier players do lots of driving. In addition, premier teams typically travel to several competitive tournaments, often out of state and sometimes out of the country.

Hybrid Soccer Programs

In different parts of the country, you may find programs that vary from those already mentioned. In some areas, for example, there are hybrid programs that fall between recreation and travel programs. Called "Challenge" soccer in North Carolina and "Rec-Plus" in Ohio and other areas, these programs offer structure and skill development with less travel and cost than travel team programs. Such leagues report better retention of players as children reach middle school age.

In other areas, some programs offer a more seamless approach. Teams organized by age are placed in divisions. The top teams are in division 1, the next best in division 2, and so on. Less competitive teams compete in lower divisions against teams of similar ability. At the end of a season, the best team or teams in each division are promoted to the next higher division. The teams with the worst records are relegated to the next lower division. This system is used in many professional leagues around the world, though it is not currently used in the U.S. pro league, Major League Soccer.

In theory, the divisional approach to organizing leagues enables teams to stay together regardless of the division in which they play. This fosters camaraderie and team spirit and develops team leaders. Weaker players are less likely to be cut. A strong player may choose to stay with average players so as to work together to achieve promotion in the future. In reality, however, unless strict policies are enforced, the best players tend to migrate to the top division teams via tryouts or recruitment. And when several top players migrate, it may cause the team they are leaving to fold.

Recently, professional soccer leagues and teams have gotten into the business of sponsoring youth teams. This is the model for youth

Viewpoint: How Would You Like to Get Cut?

The Red Lightning U-11 team my daughter plays for held tryouts recently. The tryouts are mandated by our local soccer association and overseen by a professional coaching director.

Every year there are new tryouts. Every year, girls must worry about being cut. Once again, the girls would have to win positions on the team in order to continue playing travel soccer.

For the most part, my daughter's team consists of players with average ability. A few have been blessed with exceptional athleticism. It's safe to say, though, that there are no future national-team stars on the Red Lightning.

This year, several girls who had played on the team for four seasons or more were cut. The parents of these girls were, of course, thunderstruck. They had schlepped their girls to practices, games, and tournaments all over the state and region and in all kinds of weather—week after week, year after year.

I am afraid to ask the girls who were cut how they feel. As the dad of an eleven-year-old, I can only imagine the pain and the flow of tears. I expect that many of them will not continue to play soccer.

Given this common occurrence, is it any wonder that soccer loses so many players between the ages of twelve and seventeen? A recent survey by the Soccer Industry Council of America shows that this situation is getting worse. While the number of American youngsters who play soccer continues to grow at the six- to twelve-year-old level, the number of older kids who play is declining.

This decline is the biggest problem confronting U.S. soccer today. Not the lack of qualified coaches and referees. Not the lack of media coverage. Not the demise of our professional women's league or the health of professional men's soccer. Fortunately, this is a problem that can be solved. There is no good reason to cut kids at an early age. Ban the practice. Change the way we organize leagues. Find a way to put the kids first. If we can do that, soccer's other problems will eventually solve themselves.

soccer in much of Europe and South America, but is not yet widespread in the United States. A caution about these teams: In some cases the team's name has simply been licensed to a group of entrepreneurs. The actual contact between the youth team and the parent pro club may be minimal—limited to similar uniforms and a few free tickets to games.

Criteria for Judging a Youth Soccer Program

When judging a youth soccer program, here are some questions to ask soccer administrators, parents, and children who have been involved in the program for several years. The answers should give you a better idea of what you and your child are getting into.

1. What **levels of play** are offered (tot soccer, recreation teams, travel soccer, school programs, premier and Olympic Development Program [ODP] teams), and how is the **program structured** (divisions, ABC, rec/travel/ premier)?

2. What are the **costs**? You'll want to know about all expenses, including registration fees, coaching fees, uniform costs, how often you will need to buy a new uniform, tournament registration fees, and plans for overnight travel to tournaments.

3. How is the organization's **budget** spent? Is it spent on all levels equally, such as to insure members, train referees, hire coaching directors, and build fields? Or are the fees from the recreation and travel players used to subsidize the elite teams in the organization, sending them to national or international tournaments?

4. What is the **program philosophy**? Is it to develop players and to provide a fun, low-stress experience for kids, or to bring trophies and glory to the club?

5. Are there **tryouts**? If yes, is every child placed on a team, or are some children cut? If children are cut, how is it done (dead silence or a personal call from the coach with suggestions on where to play and how to improve)?

6. Are the **most talented children** distributed evenly throughout teams in the organization, are they concentrated on elite teams, or are they placed on teams at random, such as by school district?

7. What is the **playing policy**? Will every child have an opportunity to play a significant part of the game (some groups mandate that every child play 50 percent of the game), or is this left to the coach's discretion?

8. Does the organization provide **training opportunities for coaches and referees**? Many soccer organizations will host clinics and licensing programs. Some offer certification programs on how to work with children.

9. What **level of commitment** is required on the part of players and parents? Will you be expected to volunteer time to help run the team? What are the jobs and their time requirements?

10. Where are the **practices and games** played? Are the travel times reasonable?
11. Is the **program based** in your community? Do the participants come from your neighborhood or town? Is there a meaningful opportunity for your child to meet and make friends with other kids in the program?

Youth Soccer Organizations in America

According to the latest numbers available (The Soccer Industry Council of America's 1999 National Soccer Participation Survey), 13.8 million people under age eighteen played soccer in 1998, an increase of more than 10 percent since 1987. Of those 13.8 million youth soccer players, 23 percent were first-year participants. That's quite a lot of youth soccer players looking to join an organized team. Fortunately, there are lots of youth programs to choose from.

The three national organizations are the U.S. Youth Soccer Association, the American Youth Soccer Organization, and the Soccer Association for Youth.

U.S. Youth Soccer Association (USYSA)   The U.S. Youth Soccer Association (USYSA), the youth division of the U.S. Soccer Federation, is the largest youth soccer service organization in the nation.

The USYSA registers more than 3 million youth players between the ages of five and nineteen. The nonprofit organization is made up of fifty-five member state associations—one in each state and two each in California, New York, Ohio, Pennsylvania, and Texas. The USYSA develops and administers both recreational and competitive programs, including national championships, in several age categories.

USYSA programs emphasize fun and deemphasize winning at all costs. Small-sided games are encouraged for players under ten. The organization's mission is to foster the physical, mental, and emotional growth and development of America's youth through the sport of soccer at all levels of age and competition.

The USYSA prides itself on providing a fun, safe, and healthy game for all kids: "Big kids, little kids, tall kids, short kids, young kids, older kids, kids who want to play for one season, kids who want to play for twenty seasons, kids who play strictly for fun, kids who want to compete at the highest level possible. Our programs are aimed at meeting the different needs of ALL KIDS."

The USYSA's pledge to reach "all kids" is evident in TOPSoccer (The Outreach Program for Soccer), a program for children with physical or mental disabilities. Started almost a decade ago, the training and team-placement program for boys and girls aged eight through nineteen operates in a number of communities across the country. Children in wheelchairs can even participate in TOPSoccer; the program has able-bodied children use wheelchairs, as well. With other accommodations, the game can be made accessible to children with other physical disabilities, as well as to those with mental disabilities.

For those players with advanced skills and greater ambition, highly competitive leagues are offered. The USYSA runs the Olympic Development Program (ODP), a national identification and development program for high-level players, usually between the ages of twelve and nineteen.

No matter what level of soccer you think your child is ready for, the USYSA probably has an appropriate team. Be aware, however, that the policies of USYSA clubs may vary from state to state and from league to league. Playing-time policies, for example, are often club mandated. Sometimes they are even left to the coaches' discretion.

To register your child, check your phone book for the number of a local club. They are typically listed by the name of your town, followed by "Soccer Association." If that doesn't work, call 800–4–SOCCER for the phone number of your USYSA state association. Ask the state association for the number of your local association or club. Fees vary according to what is provided by the local association or club.

American Youth Soccer Organization (AYSO) Like the USYSA, the American Youth Soccer Organization (AYSO) is affiliated with the U.S. Soccer Federation. Unlike USYSA, however, its policies are centrally—and more consistently—administered from its headquarters in Hawthorne, California. A nonprofit organization founded in Torrance, California, in 1964, AYSO boasts a membership of approximately 630,000 players and more than 250,000 volunteer coaches, referees, and administrators. Its largest membership is in the western states, but its programs are currently operating in forty-six states, Russia, Puerto Rico, American Samoa, and Jamaica.

AYSO offers programs to benefit all children four and a half to eighteen years of age, including but not limited to those with disabilities, children in economically disadvantaged communities, and those wishing to play college soccer.

AYSO is best known for its "everyone plays" philosophy and guarantees that each child will play at least half of every game. The organization's purpose is to "develop and deliver quality youth soccer programs where everyone builds positive character through participation in a fun, family environment." In its mission statement AYSO lists five principles: everyone plays; balanced teams; open registration; positive coaching; and good sportsmanship.

1. *Everyone plays*: Every player must play at least half of every game.
2. *Balanced teams*: At the start of each season, teams are set up as evenly balanced as possible.
3. *Open registration*: There are no tryouts. Interest and enthusiasm are the only requirements for playing.
4. *Positive coaching*: Coaches are trained and encouraged to make the extra effort to understand and offer positive help to the players, rather than use negative criticism.
5. *Good sportsmanship*: AYSO aims to create good sports on and off the field and to avoid a win-at-all-costs attitude. All of its programs are designed to instill good sportsmanship in the kids.

AYSO supports a program called "Character Counts," designed by the Josephson Institute of Ethics, to teach children virtue. The program embraces six principles: trustworthiness, respect, responsibility, fairness, caring, and citizenship.

AYSO relies on volunteers at the community level to maintain the programs. The basic community program is called a region. A region may have as few as 200 players or as many as 5,000 players grouped into girls' and boys' divisions based on age. (Regions may form coed U-6 teams for the introduction of soccer skills and techniques to the children, not for competitive purposes.) Several bordering regions make up an area. Several bordering areas make up a section. A section may cover several states, an entire state, or a portion of a state. There are no such things as "state associations" in AYSO.

AYSO has a national standard for operational procedures and playing rules, but because community needs and characteristics may differ, regions have the flexibility to satisfy their unique needs.

Highlighting AYSO's "open registration" principle is its Very Important Person (VIP) Program for children with physical or mental disabilities. Created in 1991, the VIP Program allows children with Down's syndrome, cerebral palsy, impaired sight or hearing, autism, and similar problems to play.

The VIP Program integrates its "very important players" into the rest of AYSO by using adult volunteers and player volunteers to help VIP players both on and off the field. Each player in the VIP program has a "buddy"—a parent, sibling, or friend—who keeps them oriented.

The goals of the VIP Program are for players to have fun, understand the fundamentals of the game, learn teamwork and fair play, increase positive self-esteem, become more physically fit, and meet new people. VIP teams can have as few as five players and may be coed.

Players with a high skill level may be able to participate in the College Athlete Program (CAP), which aims to make playing in college a reality for the student-athlete.

As is the case with the USYSA, you can probably find an AYSO team that meets the particular needs of your child—and your child will be in an environment that develops confidence and good sportsmanship.

To register your child, call 800–USA–AYSO. Locally determined annual fees include $11.75 per child to fund AYSO national services. Community programs exercise local autonomy, operating within the rules and regulations and bylaws as voted upon by executive members.

Soccer Association for Youth (SAY)   The Soccer Association for Youth (SAY), an affiliate member of the U.S. Soccer Federation, is a nonprofit recreational soccer organization for kids ages four through eighteen.

SAY started with forty teams in Cincinnati in 1967, but has grown to more than 6,500 rec teams for boys and girls, predominantly in Ohio. In 1999, 100,000 players were registered with SAY.

The overall objective of SAY is maximum participation with even competition at the various age levels. It stresses its "kids having fun" motto through a rather simple philosophy: Every player plays at least half of every game, with leagues forming balanced teams and divisions.

SAY was formed "to provide an organization within which children could learn and play soccer. The fact that any size player can be successful at the game and the modest expense required to field a team make it possible for many children to participate in organized competition."

As with the USYSA and AYSO, a win-at-all-costs mentality is contradictory to the basic objectives of SAY. Stacking teams and tryouts are not part of the SAY philosophy because they will not in the long run be beneficial to the vast majority of young people involved. SAY teams can be competitive, but having fun while developing skills is more important.

For those areas that desire a more competitive program in addition to their recreational program, SAY has developed the "Rec-Plus" program for players ten and older. Rec-Plus is similar to select soccer, but it keeps its roots in recreational soccer by requiring all children to play a minimum of half the game, just as all other SAY teams must do. Players for this program may be selected according to their abilities. The Rec-Plus season must not interfere with the primary rec season, and all Rec-Plus teams are formed by blind draw from a player pool to keep teams on an even playing field.

Groups that affiliate with SAY are called areas. Areas consist of one or more districts. Districts are made up of no less than four teams and are generally divided by geographic or school boundaries.

To register your child with a local SAY program, call 800–233–7291.

Soccer in the Streets (SITS) Thanks in large part to Carolyn McKenzie, youth soccer has moved beyond the suburbs and into disadvantaged neighborhoods. Soccer in the Streets (SITS), founded by McKenzie in 1989, is a national nonprofit agency that develops soccer, educational, and life-skills programs for children in public housing and other low-income communities.

SITS specializes in introducing soccer to young people while involving their parents and the community in the development and implementation of the program. McKenzie started SITS because she saw the need for a program that could develop and mold the character of young people while positively involving and affecting their families. She chose soccer because it's the world's most popular sport, it wasn't being played by children in public housing, and it had simple rules and could be played anywhere.

The success of the Atlanta program led soccer enthusiasts from other cities to inquire how they could bring the program to their own communities, and the program grew. SITS has introduced soccer to more than 100,000 inner-city youth in more than 75 U.S. cities. Boys and girls ages five through seventeen are eligible to participate in SITS-sponsored programs.

"Let's kick drugs and crime out of our communities" is the agency's motto. According to SITS, children who are busy with sports are less susceptible to drugs and gangs and tend to perform better academically. SITS goes beyond teaching young people how to kick a ball into a net; it serves as a drug and crime prevention mechanism by developing family unity and community involvement. Soccer is used as a tool to help children build character and positive self-images.

SITS children gain meaningful athletic, social, and educational experiences. The goal of the program is to advance the children's confidence and self-worth while promoting active and constructive lifestyles. In addition, the program can help to identify potentially gifted players who can be nurtured in their effort to reach the highest level of soccer proficiency.

SITS Program Overview *Soccer 101:* For beginners. Seven-session program that teaches children the basic skills of soccer and how to use these skills in fun, small-sided games. Each session ends with a scrimmage, so the children can apply what they have learned to game situations.

Mini Camp: One-day program that introduces kids to how a soccer game works (field positions, rules, game strategy, and so on).

Soccer 102: The recreational-league component of the SITS program, with small-sided teams (3v3, 4v4, 5v5). The objective is for each child to get as many touches on the ball as possible, which increases their opportunities for development.

Soccer in the Streets Cup: Annual local tournament (in July) in the cities that hold a Soccer 102 program. Small-sided teams in four age groups (6–8, 9–11, 12–14, 15–17). At the end of the league seasons, each site selects players to form all-star teams (one team in each specified age group). These all-star teams compete in the SITS Cup.

Soccer 103: Coaches identify and select the most talented players from SITS programs. These players represent SITS in competitive tournaments, soccer leagues (an AYSO or USYSA recreation league), state select teams, ODP, and so on. SITS pays all entry fees, transportation costs, and uniform expenses for the team. The 103 program has three goals: 1) to obtain scholarships for the players to attend camps and clinics; 2) to register the players in tournaments that are advanced and competitive; and 3) to showcase the players to private high schools and colleges for scholarship opportunities.

Soccer in the Streets National Cup: Annual tournament in Atlanta (in August). Teams from SITS cities are invited to compete in the following categories: 4v4, 5v5, 7v7.

Recruitment methods vary, but most of the inner-city children are approached through their churches or boys' and girls' clubs. For more information about an agency that has provided kids in some neighborhoods with an alternative to drugs, crime, and gangs, call 678–993–2113 or 770–452–0505 x113.

The Super Y-League The USL Super Y-League is a national youth soccer league created in 1999 as part of the United Soccer Leagues. Its purpose is to offer youth soccer as the "first rung of the ladder of opportunity" for players to make the long climb to Division I Major League Soccer. In past years, most elite-level players were limited to national competition with various state select teams. The Super Y-League attempts to augment high-level youth play with a top-caliber national youth league, featuring top players from all around the United States. These are exceptional athletes with technical and physical attributes that make them likely candidates to be productive players at the professional and national-team levels.

In 2002, the Super Y-League, through US Soccer and the United States Olympic Committee, was granted ODP programs to identify players for U.S. National Team Programs. The Super Y-League's sixth season included 13- to 17-year-old boys' and girls' teams from well over 100 clubs. Teams recruit players year-round. For more information on this elite-level program, call 813–963–3909.

US Club Soccer Another fast-growing organization devoted to the development of competitive soccer clubs and elite players, US Club Soccer includes over 1,200 clubs in 47 states. Teams from many of the top clubs in the U.S. compete in the U-12 to U-17 age brackets. The organization hosts various state and national tournaments for its members and is an affiliate of the United States Soccer Federation (USSF). To contact them, call 843–429–0006.

CHAPTER 4

Learning the Game: Object and Tactics

There are five critical steps to learning how to play soccer: understanding the object of the game, discovering tactics, mastering skills by perfecting techniques, maintaining fitness, and learning the rules. As mentioned earlier, the object of soccer is to put the ball into your opponent's net and to keep it out of yours. It is, of course, much more than that. Underlying this simple objective are opportunities to understand individual qualities of perseverance and leadership and group qualities of sportsmanship and teamwork.

Tactics

Tactics are the ideas players and their teammates use to move the ball forward into positions from which shots can be taken—or ways to take the ball from an opponent. Tactics drive a child's desire to learn the sport. It's the part for which the brain must be used. It is what the game is about.

Many coaches will tell you that tactics cannot be taught to young kids. They feel more comfortable demonstrating skills and believe that these tools of play must be taught before a player can even begin to think about tactics.

Perhaps coaches shy away from addressing tactics with young kids because they have a "playbook" mentality and think of tactics in terms of X's and O's and wiggly arrows. Tactics are in fact the building blocks of the game and can begin to be understood from the first moment a player tries to score a goal.

Examples of Early Tactical Thinking

Early on, players learn that it is not easy to either advance the ball or defend a goal alone; hence, the most basic tactic of all: find ways to get help from your teammates. For example, the earliest "tactic" your child may try is to kick the ball forward, chase it, and kick it again at the goal. This may work in the first few matches, but a child will soon discover that opponents adjust and quickly figure out how to stop the player who tries to go it alone.

Eventually, even very young players realize they must rely on teammates to help them advance the ball. A few kids come up with the clever idea of standing near the opponent's goal waiting for one of their

teammates to kick the ball near them so they can score. The child who realizes this shows he is thinking, so don't criticize the ploy. Soon enough, he will realize this is a limited tactic. First, defensive players learn to mark—that is, guard—the "goal hanger." Second, while the goal hanger is waiting for the ball to come to him, the players on the other team have an easier time of scoring on the opposite end of the field because they outnumber their opponents.

On defense, a child's first tactic is often to retreat to the goal and to stand in front of it, hoping to block a shot. She soon realizes that this approach stops few goals. Eventually, she discovers that it's better to try to take the ball from an opponent before she reaches the goal area. Next, she learns that trying to stop an advancing player with the help of a teammate is a lot easier than doing it alone. This leads to understanding that sometimes it is preferable to slow an opponent down so as to give a teammate time to arrive to help. And so on.

How to Teach Tactics

Tactics may be taught formally. Or, if you prefer, you can allow kids to discover them for themselves. My approach is to do a little of each. When I see that some children have discovered a way to advance the ball or to defend more effectively, I praise them and ask them to try to describe what they have learned. In this way, they become conscious of what they've done, and their teammates learn as well.

Teaching tactics must, of course, be balanced with skills instruction. Tactics give kids an incentive to work on skills, while skills give kids the ability to attempt more sophisticated tactics.

When you hear a coach say the game is the best teacher, it is another way of saying that tactics are what motivates players to improve. In much of the world, kids become very skillful with very little training because they are driven to learn the skills so they can attempt more sophisticated tactics.

Tactics are best learned in small-sided games where players are challenged to think. Whether in the backyard, during training sessions, or on game day, be sure to reward all tactical thinking with praise, even when a child's idea is not the best tactic. Do not force-feed kids with high-level tactics for which they are too young or unprepared.

Play games that require thinking to be successful, not simply athleticism or skill. During matches, take note of tactical ideas demonstrated by your child and the rest of the team. Try to talk about them afterward with your child or with the team. Remember: The excitement generated by discovering a new tactic gives kids the incentive to master the relatively less exciting skills.

Tactical Principles

Tactics are basic rules or principles that a team agrees upon. They determine how players should react in various situations and enable teams to act in unison with a single purpose. U.S. Soccer Federation coaching directors and instructors have identified general tactical principles and suggest that coaches try to instill them in their players.

There are two kinds of tactics: *offensive* (your team has the ball) and *defensive* (your team doesn't have the ball).

Offensive Tactical Principles On offense, a team strives for penetration into its opponent's half with depth, width, mobility, and finishing. *Depth* means to support the player with the ball in front and behind. *Width*

means to support to the side (square) and to the flanks (sidelines). *Mobility* means to make runs to exploit openings or imbalances in the opponent's defense. *Finishing* is getting into position to score and putting the ball in the net.

For young players—and even for many older players—tactical principles are fairly abstract and need to be translated into rules for how to act in specific situations.

On offense, I explain to players that there are three basic possibilities: You have the ball, you're near a teammate who has the ball, or you're not near the ball. In each case, there is a decision-making process that should become second nature to players.

A player who has the ball (called being the first attacker) should make one of the following moves:

1. Look to score.
2. Move the ball to a spot where scoring is possible (penetrate), either by dribbling or passing to a teammate who is moving to the goal.
3. Maintain possession by playing the ball away from pressure to a supporting teammate.

When near a teammate who has the ball (called being the second attacker, of which there can be more than one), the player should make one of the following moves:

1. Move into position to receive a pass and score a goal.
2. Lessen the pressure on the player with the ball by being available for a pass to the side, front, or behind, or by getting into position for a wall pass (give and go).
3. Combine with the first attacker to penetrate by making runs to confuse and surprise the opposition, such as check, diagonal (through), or overlapping runs or takeovers.

When not near the ball (called being the third attacker, of which there should be several), the player should make one of the following moves:

1. Open space by drawing off a defender with a longer run, thereby creating space into which another teammate may move to receive a pass.
2. Run to an open area where it's possible to receive a long pass that "changes the field" (moves play unexpectedly from one side of the field to the other).
3. Rotate to a defensive position to cover for a defender who has become involved in the attack.

Defensive Tactical Principles　On defense, the tactic is to try to regain possession as quickly as possible but without risking a goal-scoring opportunity for the other team. To do so, players give immediate chase and delay the attacking team with depth, balance, and concentration. *Immediate chase* means to quickly close down on and slow the progress of the player with the ball. *Depth*, here, means to move into defensive positions in front and in back of the attacking players. *Balance* means to mark or cover players away from the ball who are in a position to penetrate. *Concentration*, or compactness, is achieved when the attacker's options have been limited or eliminated, allowing defenders to tackle, intercept, or win a loose ball.

When explaining these principles to players, it is helpful to break them down into rules. Once again, there are three possibilities:

The player who is nearest to the opponent with the ball (called being the first defender) should make one of the following moves:

1. Immediately get goalside (between the attacker and your goal) and delay the attacking player from advancing.
2. Deny penetration, especially to the center of the field. (Try to channel—that is, move—the attacker to the outside.)
3. When support arrives, apply pressure and win the ball with a tackle if possible.

When near the ball but not the closest player (called being the second defender, of which there can be several), the player should make one of the following moves:

1. Support a teammate who is trying to get the ball back.
2. Eliminate the attacker's best passing option.

When not near the player with the ball (called being one of the third defenders), the player should make one of the following moves:

Key Tactical Concepts for Young Players

On offense:

- Use simple passes with a high probability of completion throughout most of the field.

- Keep dribbling to a minimum, especially in your defensive zone.

- Near the goal, it's OK to dribble or try a risky pass if necessary to surprise opponents and create a scoring opportunity.

- Dominate time of possession and there is a better chance to score. It is also less likely your team will be scored upon. Short passes are the best way to maintain possession.

- Use long passes to vary the attack, surprise opponents, and to make use of teammates with exceptional speed.

- Move the ball away from pressure to open areas as you attempt to penetrate.

- Get one or more players with the ball behind your opponent's defenders to create scoring opportunities.

- Use teammates who have exceptional skill. For example, get the ball to the player who has the best chance to score; or, get the ball to the player who can "hold" the ball and make dangerous passes.

- Don't waste restarts. Take corner kicks and both indirect and direct free kicks quickly and with a plan.

- Once it's clear the ball will turn over, switch to defense. A delay of even one or two seconds can make a big difference.

On defense:

- Have more defenders between the ball and the goal (don't be outnumbered when opponents attack).

- Try to channel (move) the attacker with the ball away from the center of the field.

- Build out of the back (move the ball through the defensive third) by playing the ball to the flanks (outside) and then upfield.

- Clear the ball from the goal area by kicking it as high, wide, and deep as possible.

- Under dangerous pressure, it's OK to kick the ball out of play.

- Initiate the attack immediately upon winning a turnover.

- Work with your goalkeeper to build defensive walls. Defend threatening restarts quickly and with purpose.

1. Move to a place where the team's defense is weak, especially if it's in the center of the field.
2. Cover or mark opponents who make runs into attacking positions.

Playing Positions

Positions in small-sided soccer may be as simple as "attacker" when your team has the ball and "defender" when it doesn't. As kids graduate to 6v6 or 8v8, it's helpful to assign more specific roles, such as right attacker, left midfielder, or center defender. Once kids are playing with eleven players per side, positions become still more refined.

Keep in mind, however, that positions in soccer are not carved in stone as they are in baseball, basketball, football, and other sports. Although positions generally define roles and areas of play, a great amount of freedom is given to each player. A forward may retreat to help on defense. A defender may make a run and score or help score a goal.

On some teams, players are expected to adopt positional roles on an ad hoc or improvisational basis. A flank midfielder or central defender may rotate into a forward's position, and the forward may move into a more withdrawn position during the attack. Such a system requires a high level of experience, training, and communication.

Most youth teams use a more structured approach to positions. The forwards stay forward with some defensive responsibility in the midfield. The defenders stay back, making forward runs only occasionally.

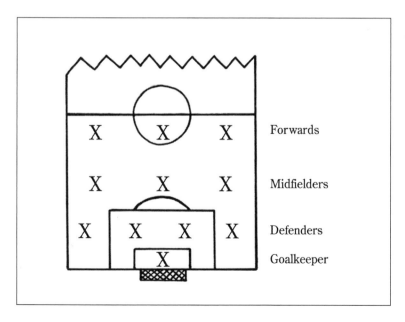

Figure 4.1: A 4-3-3 formation is one of the most common formations in youth soccer.

Positions for Children Playing Full-Sided (11v11) Soccer

Center forward

Key skills: Dribbling, shooting, one-touch passing, turning, 1v1 moves.

Key attributes: Quickness, timing, courage, and creativity.

Primary duties: To score goals.

Outside forwards

Key skills: Shooting, crosses, and corner kicks; one-touch passing; 1v1 moves.

Key attributes: Speed and timing.

Primary duties: To assist in the scoring of goals.

Center midfielder

Key skills: Receiving, dribbling, passing, chipping, long shots, 1v1 moves.

Key attributes: Vision, quickness, leadership.

Primary duties: Distribute ball to players who penetrate; assist on offense and defense.

Outside midfielders

Key skills: Passing, long shots and crosses, throwing.

Key attributes: Speed, endurance.

Primary duties: Help move ball from defense to attack, assist on offense and defense, open field by being a passing option for defenders, midfielders, and forwards.

Central defenders

Key skills: Tackling, passing, heading, long passes, and clearing.

Key attributes: Strength, speed, endurance, stability, determination.

Primary duties: Stop penetration by attackers, pass ball to open midfielders, goal kicks.

Outside defenders

Key skills: Tackling, long passes and clearing, throwing.

Key attributes: Strength, speed, endurance, stability.

Primary duties: Keep attackers from penetrating center of field, pass ball to open midfielders, open up the field by being a safe outside passing option for goalkeepers and central defenders.

Goalkeeper

Key skills: Catching, diving, throwing, punting, long kicks, receiving.

Key attributes: Strength, good hands, jumping ability, courage, good communication, concentration.

Primary duties: Save balls from entering the net; organize the defense, especially for free kicks; goal kicks; initiate attacks with intelligent ball distribution.

And the midfielders try to link up the defenders and forwards and generally help out on both ends of the field. Nevertheless, it's important for children to understand that a broad definition of positions can be advantageous to a team.

Typical Soccer Formations

Once your child begins to play full-sided soccer, you'll probably begin to hear the word *formations*. With this word, there will be numerical sequences, such as 4-4-2 and 3-4-3. These combinations tell you how players are deployed on the field. The first number refers to the number of defenders, the second to midfielders, and the third to forwards or attackers. The numbers are always listed from defense to offense, so a 4-3-3 means there are four defenders, three midfielders, and three forwards. Since there is always one goalkeeper, that position is not included in the designations.

The most common formations in youth soccer are 4-3-3 at the younger ages and 4-4-2 at older ages.

Formations go in and out of style. When I played in high school, the almost universal formation was 2-3-5. Our five attackers were center, right and left inners, and right and left outers. Early versions of the game relied on a 9-1 formation!

A coach who feels outmatched may choose a more defensive formation for a team, such as a 4-4-2, or even a 4-5-1.

The numbers do not tell the whole story. A 4-4-2, for instance, may be made up of left and right defenders, a stopper (first player to the ball on defense), and a sweeper (last player on defense). Or the same formation may have a flat or level back four, with four defenders each responsible for their areas.

With young children, it's not wise to put too much emphasis on formations. If a child understands the need to pay attention to a particular side of the field on attack or defense, that's enough.

Advanced Tactics

In addition to general tactical principles described in the preceding sections, coaches will often add tactics based on the strengths and weaknesses of their teams or of an opposing team. For example, if a team has forwards who are outstanding at heading balls, the tactic may be to target the forwards by serving balls into the penalty area whenever possible. An outmatched team may choose to focus primarily on defense and rely upon one speedy forward to score on a quick counterattack.

Or, a team may take advantage of the offside trap (where defenders step forward to put attackers in offside positions) to make it tougher for opponents to penetrate their defensive third of the field. While advanced tactics are not usually introduced until children play on older youth teams, it's good for a parent to have some understanding of them for when a child asks questions. They are also fun to discuss while watching professional and international matches—another great way to see examples of tactics at work.

Games That Teach Tactics

Tactics, especially for younger players, are best taught through the use of games. The games listed below are a small sampling of the many available to you. See the "Books" and "Videos" sections in appendix C for additional sources.

Keep-Away The simple game of keep-away in a confined area is a good way to illustrate the fundamental tactics of possession, depth, and mobility. Place three players in a 10-yard square and suggest that two of them try to keep the ball from the third. The two with the ball will quickly learn that getting open for a pass is a fundamental tactic. Properly executed, it makes it very difficult for the lone player to win the ball.

Two vs. three players with the ball is even more instructive. Now, defenders have more tactical choices. While one applies pressure on the

Figure 4.2:
"Keep-Away" game. Adjust the size of the playing area according to the skill level and number of players.

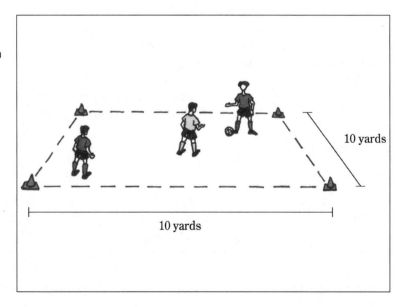

10 yards

10 yards

player with the ball, the other must decide which receiver to cover. If thinking tactically, the free defender will cover the one in the best position to receive a pass. The pressuring player, if thinking tactically, may also be able to apply pressure and cut off a passing channel at the same time.

With a larger group, you may enlarge the field of play and add several small goals made from cones. This adds the tactical dimension

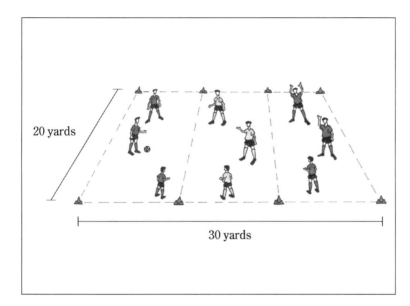

Figure 4.3: "Team-in-the-Middle" game.

20 yards

30 yards

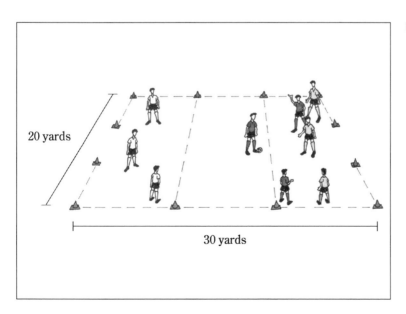

Figure 4.4: "Three-Team" game.

20 yards

30 yards

of penetration. Players may score in either direction. You may add the further challenge of counting the goal only when a shot passes through a goal and is received by a teammate.

Team-in-the-Middle   This game is similar to monkey-in-the-middle, but with teams. The object is to stay out of the middle; there are no goals.

Divide a 20-by-30-yard area into three equal areas. Mark the areas with cones. Divide players into three equal teams. Put one team into each area.

Give the ball to one of the teams at either end of the field. The two end teams try to play the ball through the middle zone without losing the ball to the team in the middle. Balls may be played on the ground or in the air. Players may not leave their zones during play.

If the middle team wins the ball, it changes places with the team that last played the ball. If an end team plays the ball out of bounds, it exchanges places with the team in the middle.

Encourage players to think about positions—keeping some players forward and others back, for example—and passing to where it's easier to send the ball across the middle.

Three-Team Soccer   In this game, there are goals, just as in real soccer. Otherwise, the setup is identical to team-in-the-middle. The object, however, is to stay in the middle of the field.

How to play: Give the ball to the team in the middle and allow them to choose which end team to attack. The middle team may then enter the end team's zone and try to score a goal. The end team may not, however, enter the middle zone. If the attacking team scores, they may return to the middle and attack the team at the other end. If a defending end team is able to steal the ball and send it into the middle area, it wins and takes over as the middle team. The team that scores the most goals wins.

Once again, encourage players to decide on positions and tactics among themselves.

CHAPTER 5

Skills and Techniques

Skills are essential for players to implement tactics. Players who can pass accurately and receive the ball with confidence, for example, can develop a much wider repertoire of tactics than those who cannot. Unfortunately, skills are not much fun to learn—certainly not as much fun as playing the game. They take a lot of practice. That means doing the same thing over and over. In this chapter and in the one that follows on goalkeeping, you'll find a catalog of skills with some clues as to how to execute them properly.

Don't—I repeat, *don't*—expect a young child to have much interest in watching you demonstrate the skills shown. Instead, build games around the skills. Although I suggest games for the skills described in detail in this chapter, feel free to develop your own games with your kids.

The Skills Groups

There are hundreds of soccer skills, but they fall into seven basic groups:

Shooting Skills The favorite skill of almost all young players is shooting. It's arguably also the most important of all skills—passing, dribbling, and all the rest are useless unless someone on the team can shoot balls past the keeper and into the goal. There are many ways to shoot a ball. They include the instep drive, side volley, half volley, full volley, jump header, diving header, bicycle kick, and scissors kick, as well as many variations you have to make up on the spot, such as the toe poke and sliding toe poke.

Passing Skills Some players feel that passes are the most beautiful part of the game. This is not because passing skills are difficult to master. It's because passes reveal the thinking part of the game. They show that a masterful player knows where the rest of the team is and the best place to play the ball in order to create or deny a scoring opportunity. Experienced players almost seem to read their teammates' minds to create incredible passing combinations. Passing skills include one- and two-touch push passes, long driven passes, crosses, chips, headed passes, and heel passes, as well as many variations.

Receiving Skills Receiving was once called trapping. But coaching instructors have decided that "trap" may give young players the wrong idea. Even this new label is not a good description of this highly critical skill. To receive is really a series of acts beginning with gaining control of the ball, usually a passed ball, and then preparing to play the ball. Receiving a ball can be done with any part of the body except the hands or arms, but is most frequently done with various parts of the feet, the inside of the knees or thighs, or with the chest.

Dribbling Skills Dribbling involves moving the ball by tapping it with any part of either foot in any direction. Watching a good dribbler move past defenders is the most exciting part of the game, aside from seeing a goal scored. Some coaches discourage dribbling because it often leads to turnovers. Consequently, the United States produces relatively few superb dribblers. Today, however, most top-level coaches believe that young players should be encouraged to dribble more, even if it means occasional loss of the ball. As players reach eight or nine years of age, dribbling should be discouraged near a player's own goal, commonly called the defensive third of the field, because a turnover here often results in a goal.

Defensive Skills This large group of skills allows a player to do several things, depending upon the situation. *Marking* (covering), for example, is how to position yourself next to an opponent so as to have the best opportunity to intercept a pass or get into a position to prevent the attacker's progress to the goal. *Channeling* allows you to move or guide a player toward the sidelines, where the options are fewer and the possibility of scoring is decreased. Tackling is a way to win 50-50 balls (the ones that you and your opponent have an equal chance to possess). These skills are important for all players, regardless of position.

Fakes and Moves Although fakes and moves may be considered extensions of the dribbling skill, it's helpful to learn them individually. A *fake* is any ploy used by a player to win time and space from an opponent. For example, a fake shot or pass usually causes a defending player to move in a way that will block the shot or pass. This allows the player with the ball time to consider other options. A *move*, often called a 1v1 move, is a combination of body and foot feints aimed at allowing the player with the ball to get behind the defending player. Use 1v1 moves when beating an opponent while going to the goal. Moves are used much less frequently in the defensive third of the field than in the middle and offensive thirds.

There are many moves, but they all can be reduced to body and foot fakes, with or without the ball (that is, where the ball is moved in a way to fake the defender or where just the body is moved). For example, moves where the ball is "offered" include moving the ball in the opposite direction you intend to take it, pulling it back or pushing it aside, and then accelerating in a different direction. Cutting, on the other hand, involves leaning or lunging your body in the opposite direction you intend to take the ball and then accelerating in the intended direction.

Wiel Coerver has identified many moves and described them for use in his Coerver Coaching Method. He observed the moves of professional players and developed teaching materials so that kids can learn how to execute the moves and use them in matches. See the video titled *A New Era*, described in appendix C.

Throw-Ins Throw-ins are how balls are put back into play when they go outside either sideline. To be successful with throw-ins, a player needs coordination, strength, and an understanding of the throw-in rule—a tall order for a young child. For this reason, don't make a big deal of improper throw-ins with young kids. Refs should not call infractions either, unless it's obvious that the child is intentionally breaking the rules to gain advantage—such as throwing the ball with one arm.

Techniques

Technique is often used interchangeably with skill, but there is a difference. Techniques are prescribed ways to move the body in order to execute skills effectively and consistently. A highly skilled player is said to have good technique. For example, shooting the ball is a skill. One shooting technique is to run straight at the ball and blast it with the toe. Is it a good technique? Many young kids will argue that it is (especially if the ball is soft or underinflated) because they can make the ball go faster and farther than with other parts of the shoe.

Another technique is to shoot with the instep (the top of the foot, often referred to as the laces since most shoes fasten there). Shooting the ball with the laces is commonly accepted as good technique, while kicking with the toe is usually considered poor technique. One approach delivers more consistent results than the other—and hurts less. Good technique will allow a player to shoot the ball straight most of the time. Technique may also include the approach to the ball, where the ball is struck, lean of the body, placement of the non-kicking foot, and the direction in which the follow-through is made.

Level I Skills

Level I skills may be taught to children once they begin to play organized soccer, at six or seven years old. Keep in mind when introducing

Aim your supporting foot in direction of kick.

more difficult skills that a child who is not "getting it" is probably not developmentally ready for those skills. Avoid creating frustration and simply reintroduce the skills at a later date. There are no prizes for being the first to learn all the skills.

Instep Drive   The instep drive is a basic way to shoot the ball that kids should learn early on. A hard, low shot, it can be used from outside the goal area or closer in if it's done quickly. Learning this shot also provides a good foundation for learning how to drive long passes and to make goal kicks.

What to Show Your Child
1. Approach the ball from a slight angle so you can swing your body and get more power when you kick.
2. Run to the ball with short steps. Short steps will enable a child to time the last step so . . .
3. . . . the non-kicking foot winds up about 8 to 12 inches to the side of the ball.
4. Bring your kicking foot behind your body.

5. Swing your foot forward from the hip and knee.

6. With your body and knee nearly over the ball . . .

7. . . . strike the ball with your instep (see photo). Your ankle should be stiff and your toe pointed down.

8. Follow through in the direction of the kick, with your foot staying low.

9. Land on your non-kicking foot.

Tips Aim your non-kicking foot in the direction you want the ball to go. Aim to strike the center of the ball.

Backyard Game Set up two goals in the backyard and suggest that one child guard one goal and a second guard the other. The goals can be made with cones or rags—anything that will not cause injury should the child fall on it. The size of the goal and distance between goals depends upon the age and strength of the children. Allow the children to take turns shooting at each other's goal. The child who scores a preselected number of goals first wins—and must defend a goal one step wider in the next game.

Strike the center of the ball with your instep.

Push Pass The most basic pass—and the one that's used most frequently—is called the push pass. It's done with the inside of either foot and is accurate and useful for short- to medium-range passing. You may take two touches (one to stop the ball and one to pass it) or one touch (both stopping and passing the ball; a Level II skill described in the next section) to make a push pass.

What to Show Your Child

1. Prepare the ball (put the ball where you can easily strike it) by pushing it forward a few feet in a direction that gives you time and distance from the nearest opponent.

2. When under pressure, the best preparation for passing may be a fake pass. Fake moving or passing in one direction and then push the ball in a different direction to prepare the pass.

3. Step quickly to the ball. Don't give opponents time to react and block your pass!
4. Plant your non-kicking foot a few inches from the ball, knee bent and toes pointing in the direction you want the pass to go.
5. Turn your passing foot so it's almost perpendicular to the direction of the pass and strike the ball firmly with the inside of your foot.
6. Follow through in the direction of the pass.
7. Move off to put yourself into a new, advantageous position in which to receive the ball.

Strike the ball center with the inside of the foot and make a full follow-through.

Tips Some kids have trouble with the push pass at first because they attempt it from a standstill with the ball close to their feet. Show how you must step to the ball, body leaning slightly back, in order to make the pass with power. Then tell your child to drive through the center of the ball using the inside of the foot, but as though the heel was driving through the ball on the follow-through.

Backyard Game Young players enjoy soccer croquet. It requires two or three people and one ball. Have two players stand about 10 to 20 yards apart. Stand between them and spread your legs. Ask each player to pass the ball through your legs. If the ball misses or hits a leg, that player must take your place. Change the distance between players or how wide you spread your legs to adjust the difficulty to match the skill of the players. An additional challenge is to have kids make push passes first with one foot and then with the other. It's important to develop comfort passing with either foot.

Receiving Rolling Balls The simplest and most useful reception is with the inside of the foot. It is the first receiving skill your child should learn. Not only does it make it possible to stop the ball with confidence, but it also keeps the ball close in front where it can be played quickly and easily.

What to Show Your Child

1. Face the passer so that it is clear you are ready to receive the ball.
2. If an opponent is close by, move toward the ball to give yourself more time to receive it.
3. Turn your leg so your foot is perpendicular to the path of the pass.
4. Put your weight on the non-receiving foot and slightly bend the knee on that side.
5. Raise the toes of the receiving foot to create a bigger area for receiving the ball.
6. Upon contact with the ball, allow the foot to "give" or pull back so the ball stays close to your feet.
7. Prepare to play the ball by tapping it forward or, to reverse direction, by pulling it back with the sole of the shoe.

Receive the ball with the inside of the foot and push it in the direction you want to play it next.

Tips Show your child the arch of the foot and explain that this is what players use to "catch" the ball. Work with your child to develop comfort in receiving the ball with either foot. Once a child is comfortable receiving the ball without letting it bounce away, demonstrate how to make the next touch. Tactically, this should usually be *away* from pressure. For now, it is enough to be able to tap the ball in an intended direction upon receiving it.

Backyard Game Place one child in the center of a circle of friends or siblings. Have the kids in the circle pass the ball to the child in the center. This child must receive each pass, prepare it for a return pass, and then make passes to each child in the ring. Once the kids have become comfortable executing the passes and receptions, add excitement by timing how long it takes each of them to complete the cycle. The goal of the group is to complete the cycle in the least amount of time, trying to set a new "record" each time. If no other kids are available, place cones in a circle and serve passes to the child yourself. Ask the child to receive each pass and to then make passes at each cone. It helps to have a supply of balls to keep this game moving. Increase

Stop the ball with the outside of your foot and "prepare" it for your next touch by tapping it away from pressure (opponents).

the challenge by enlarging the circle and setting goals for how quickly the circuit is made.

Outside-of-the-Foot Reception Similar to receiving a rolling ball with the inside of the foot, the outside-of-the-foot reception allows players to receive and redirect the ball away from an opponent in a single touch. A player may use either foot—the right foot for cutting to the right, and the left foot for cutting to the left. Add a fake by dipping your shoulder in the direction opposite to the one you're heading to freeze your defending opponent.

What to Show Your Child

1. Move to the oncoming ball quickly so your opponent has less time to attempt an interception.
2. Place your non-receiving foot parallel to the ball's path and slightly behind it (closer to you).
3. With your weight on your non-receiving foot and knee bent, lean opposite to the direction you will move in order to deceive your opponent.
4. Raise your receiving foot to mid-ball height.
5. As it makes contact, push the ball in the opposite direction of your fake.
6. Move off with the ball, eyes up.

Tips Do not strike the ball hard upon receiving it. Keep it near you and away from the players marking you.

Backyard Game Use the same game as for "Receiving Rolling Balls," except the child in the middle must receive with the outside of the foot.

Basic Dribbling Dribbling is usually done while the player is moving forward with speed, but can be done in any direction and at various speeds. Moves and fakes are used with dribbling to get past opponents or to create time and space in which to play the ball.

What to Show Your Child

1. Push the ball forward with different parts of the foot: toe, inside, outside, top (instep), and sole.
2. Push the ball to either side with different parts of the foot.
3. Pull the ball backward using the inside, outside, sole, and heel.
4. When dribbling with a defender nearby, use small taps to keep the ball close to you and away from the defender.

To dribble, you may use the instep, . . .

. . . the outside of the foot, . . .

. . . the inside of the foot, . . .

. . . and the sole of the shoe.

5. Speed dribbling—when no defender is near, such as on a breakaway—allows the dribbler to make stronger taps on the ball and to push it farther ahead.

Tips   Dribble with your head up—not down—so you can see your teammates and defenders. Use your low peripheral vision (the bottom edge of your field of vision) to check the progress of the ball. Without good field vision, you will not know where to play the ball next. Throw off defenders by varying dribbling speed, and dribble with the foot that is farthest from the defender so that your body protects the ball from being stolen.

Backyard Game   For groups of five to seven young children, place four cones to create a 10- or 15-yard square. Ask the kids to dribble in the square without bumping into each other. Once kids can dribble with some control and without collisions, tell them you're going to toss or roll balls into the square and that they must avoid being touched by them. You may ask those who are touched by a ball to dribble the ball around the outside of the square. This drill, devised by Ron Quinn, national youth coaching director for U.S. Soccer, is an excellent way to make dribbling fun and to force kids to look up while dribbling. For additional games, see Ron Quinn's book, *The Peak Performance*, listed in appendix C.

Backyard Game   Set two targets, such as trash cans or picnic benches, 15 to 20 yards apart. Two players take turns using moves to try to pass each other and shoot at the target. Score one point each time a player uses a move successfully and one point if the target is hit.

Short Throw-Ins   Short throw-ins are the norm in soccer, even at advanced levels. The aim is to put the ball in play and to maintain possession. Short throw-ins are often made to a player who runs to the thrower and away from a marking player. If pressured, the receiver has the option of playing the ball back to the thrower.

What to Show Your Child
1. Decide where you will throw the ball.
2. Stand behind the line and grip the sides of the ball with fingers spread.
3. Raise the ball over your head and behind your neck, bending your arms.

4. Swing your arms forward and release the ball toward your target.

5. Follow through with both hands.

Tips Many refs will insist that the ball be retracted behind the head before throwing it. They also watch to see that you use both arms to throw rather than favoring one. Do not step past the sideline or raise either foot from the turf until after you release the ball. To gain advantage, short throw-ins should be taken quickly to an unmarked teammate. Delays enable opponents to mark you and your teammates.

Backyard Game Take turns with your child throwing the ball at a target marked on a wall or rebounder. To start, stand behind a line that is 6 or 7 yards from the target. Make the target low, to simulate throwing to the feet of a teammate. Score one point for hitting the target and zero for a miss. Make the game more challenging by lengthening the distance to the target and varying the angle of the throw.

Level II Skills

Level II skills are typically focused upon once a child reaches nine or ten years of age.

One-Touch Push Passes Players should use the one-touch pass if they are under pressure from opponents or if an advantage can be gained by passing the ball quickly. The one-touch push pass is more difficult to strike accurately than a pass executed with two touches, but with

Approach the pass and point your supporting foot in the direction you want to make the pass.

Strike the oncoming pass with your ankle locked and your toes raised slightly.

practice it can be mastered by young children. It is the best way to frustrate defenders and move the ball to your opponent's goal. It is also a great way to keep rough physical teams at bay. If you use one-touch passes, your opponents will never get close enough to you to commit a foul.

What to Show Your Child
1. Approach the moving ball with short quick steps.
2. Place your non-kicking foot a few inches to the side of where the ball will be when you strike it.
3. Bend the knee of the non-kicking (supporting) leg as you retract the kicking foot.
4. Swing the kicking foot forward, turning toes outward and higher than your ankle.
5. Lock your ankle and strike the middle of the ball.
6. Follow through with the kicking ankle locked and toes out.

Tips Look for teammates you can pass to *before* you receive the ball. When opponents are near, move toward oncoming passes to allow you more time to handle them—and to give opponents less time to beat you to the ball.

Backyard Game Lay two picnic benches on their sides, seat to seat, and 15 to 20 yards apart. Mark a target on each bench. Position a player with a ball between the benches. Ask the player to use the push pass to try to hit the target on one bench, to receive the rebound, and to try to hit the opposite target with the next push pass. Score one point for each time the target is hit.

Long Kicks Often called drives, long kicks are used for many purposes in soccer, including goal kicks, long passes, corner kicks, long shots, and free kicks.

What to Show Your Child
1. Run to the ball at a slight angle to the direction of the kick.
2. As you get close to the ball, shorten your steps so you can plant your non-kicking foot without overrunning the ball.
3. As you plant your non-kicking foot a few inches to the side and slightly behind the ball . . .
4. . . . bring your kicking foot back . . .
5. . . . and swing your leg forward from the hip and the knee.

6. Strike below the center of the ball with your instep. Your toes should be slightly lower than your heel.
7. Make a long, high follow-through in the direction of the kick.

Tips Keep your ankle locked as you make the kick. The lower you strike the ball, the higher it will go. For longer kicks, lengthen your run to the ball and lengthen the backswing of your kicking leg.

To drive a ball, place your supporting foot slightly behind the ball and strike it low with the instep, toes slightly lower than the heel.

Backyard Game This is a simple and fun game for equally matched children or for parent and child. In a large field, stand about 20 yards apart. One player kicks the ball as far as possible in the direction of the other player. The second player receives the ball as close to where it lands as possible, and then tries to kick it back to the first player. If the ball reaches the first player in the air or goes beyond him, score one point for the kicker. If not, no points are awarded. Play until one player scores ten points.

Long Throw-Ins Long throw-ins, typically taken by the outside midfielder, are often used to gain advantage in the attacking half of the field. The long throw-in is especially dangerous because the receiving attacker need not be in an onside position to receive it.

What to Show Your Child
1. Find your target. It may be a teammate who has run to open space.
2. Step back to give yourself space for a running start.
3. Grip the sides of the ball with two hands, slightly to the back of the ball.
4. Run forward. As you near the sideline, bring the ball behind your neck.
5. Bend your knees, arms, and wrists and arch your back.
6. Bring the ball forward swiftly and release it. Extend arms forward.
7. Follow through by swinging arms down and bringing your feet together.

Tip For extra distance in your throw, snap your wrists forward as you release the ball.

Backyard Game With three players, give one (the thrower) several balls. Make a second player the receiver and the last, the defender. The object is for the thrower to complete a thrown-in pass to the receiver without the defender poking it away or controlling it. A defender who intercepts one of three throws becomes the thrower, and the thrower becomes the defender. If the defender misses three in a row, the thrower and receiver change places, and the new thrower takes three chances.

Chipping A chipped ball travels a relatively short distance. It is usually used to send the ball over the head of a defender and drop it at the feet of an attacking teammate. Sometimes it is used to score goals when a keeper has advanced off the line and the shooter sends the ball over the keeper's head into the goal.

Using a short backswing . . .

. . . strike the ball with a stabbing kick.

End with a short follow-through.

What to Show Your Child

1. Approach the ball with short steps.
2. Plant your non-kicking foot beside the ball about 8 to 10 inches away, toes pointing in the direction you want the ball to go.
3. Using a short backswing, stab at the bottom of the ball with the toe.
4. Make contact with the lower portion of the instep.
5. Limit your follow-through.

Tip Kick with the knee, not from the hip.

Backyard Game Set a large container such as a trash barrel in the center of a 20-yard-square open area. Suggest a chipping game where players receive one point for scoring a "basket" from 5 yards away, two points from 10 yards away, and three points from 15 yards away.

Marking Marking or covering an opposing player is the most basic of defensive skills. When the other team has the ball and you are not near the player who has it, you should look to find an opponent to mark.

To *mark* means to position yourself in such a way as to have the best chance of intercepting a pass or stopping an opponent who is likely to receive a pass. This position is usually behind and central to the man you are marking. In general, mark closely if the man you're marking is close to the ball. For players far from the ball, you may mark more loosely.

What to Show Your Child

1. Position yourself so you can see the player you are marking and the ball at the same time.
2. Stand parallel or sideways to the anticipated path of the pass so you can easily move forward or back.
3. If the ball is played to your man, your first goal should be to try to intercept the ball.
4. If you are unable to win the ball cleanly, such as on a 50-50 ball, try to apply enough pressure so you force your opponent to misplay the ball or you are able to poke the ball away.
5. If you have no chance to win the ball or break up the play, get close enough to the player to prevent him from turning to face the goal.
6. Slow your opponent until you have teammates to help you force a turnover.

Try to win the ball outright, if possible. Here, the defender steps in front of the pass to intercept the ball.

If you cannot win the ball outright, disrupt the play by poking the ball away.

If neither of the above is possible, prevent your opponent from turning.

Tip If your opponent has received a pass, stay so close (within arm's length) that it's difficult for the player to spin and turn on you without losing the ball.

Backyard Game Tie a 15-foot string between two players and position them inside an area about 15 yards square. Have them take turns trying to break the string while staying within the area. The first player to score five wins. If one player is faster than the other, make the string longer when that player is on offense (being marked).

Standing Tackle The standing tackle is designed to take the ball away from an opponent using the foot. The tackle is used when a defender feels confident of support (backup) from one or more teammates should the tackle fail.

What to Show Your Child

1. Position yourself sideways and to the inside of an oncoming opponent who is dribbling the ball.

2. Fall back as the dribbler approaches. Try to maintain about 2 yards between you and the ball, more if he is dribbling very fast.

3. Try to slow the progress of the dribbler by feigning the tackle. If the dribbler slows down, close the distance between you and the ball.

4. When you have one or more supporting players (players backing you up), attempt to block the progress of the ball with your foot.

5. Once you have contacted the ball with your foot, move your body behind it to keep your opponent from simply pushing past you and to prevent the ball from bouncing off your opponent and past you.

6. Attempt to gain control of the ball or to poke it to a supporting teammate.

Tips The best time to tackle is immediately after your opponent has touched the ball forward, especially when it's gotten out too far ahead. Be ready for the dribbler to cut the ball away from the direction of your tackle. The dribbler may cut in the opposite direction (in which case you may have to attempt the tackle with your trailing foot) or may attempt to push past you in the direction of your tackle (in which case you have a good chance of winning the ball if you are fast).

Defender (right) times his tackle for when the dribbler taps the ball too far forward.

Keeping your body behind ball, jar the ball loose by contacting it with the inside of your foot and holding your foot on the ball until attacker's momentum carries her off it.

The dribbler's other option is to pull the ball back and retreat, in which case you've accomplished your goal of stopping the attacker's forward movement and reduced the opposition's passing options.

Backyard Game Have two players face each other with the ball between them at their feet. The ball should be touching the inside of each player's foot. On a signal, such as the count of three, each player tries to advance the ball. The first player to move the ball forward 1 yard wins. Restart with opposite feet. You may also drop the ball between two players to begin the action. Point out that the player who is able to keep a foot on the ball longest often wins possession.

Time your reception so your foot contacts the ball about 1 foot above ground level.

Receiving Long Passes with the Foot

Controlling all kinds of balls is imperative to becoming a strong soccer player. Many balls arrive in the air and are received with the foot. This skill requires good judgment and a soft touch.

What to Show Your Child

1. Move into a position so the approaching ball would land in front of you.

"Give" with your receiving foot at contact . . .

. . . and allow the ball to drop at your feet.

2. Balance your weight on your non-receiving leg, knee slightly bent.
3. Lift the foot with which you will receive the ball about 1 foot off the ground, in line with the falling ball.
4. Hold the receiving foot level with the ground.
5. Upon contact, "give" with your foot and leg to cushion the impact and to prevent the ball from bouncing away.
6. Dribble away, or prepare the ball for a pass.

Tip If you perform this skill correctly, the ball will roll off your foot.

Backyard Game Mark a 5-foot-diameter circle on the driveway, playground, or street with chalk, or mark a circle on the lawn using lime. One player stands in the center of the circle, and the server tosses high balls to her. She must receive the ball using either foot without allowing the ball to roll or bounce outside the circle.

Receiving with the Chest As a child gets older and the play becomes faster, ball control is essential. Controlling the ball with the chest gives the receiving player more time with the ball—saving the time it takes to step back and receive the ball with the feet and keeping the ball away from the feet of defenders. Receiving the ball with the chest is often a safe alternative to clearing balls with the head.

Girls should receive the ball above the breasts.

Boys should receive the ball on the muscled part of the chest.

What to Show Your Child

1. Move into a position where you can stop the ball with your chest.
2. Bend your knees and arch your back as the ball approaches.
3. Allow the ball to hit the muscled area of the chest, not the sternum (bone in the center of the chest). Girls may want to use the chest area that is above the breasts to stop the ball.
4. Upon impact, pull your chest back slightly to cushion the impact of the ball.
5. As the ball hits the ground, use your feet to move the ball away from pressure and in the direction you want to go.

Tips Upon striking the chest, the ball should pop off the chest and land at your feet—not several feet away, where it will probably be intercepted. When being tightly marked (covered), don't wait for the ball to reach the ground before moving it in the direction you want to go. Instead, direct the ball by pushing it with one side of the chest or the other.

Backyard Game Mark a 5-foot-diameter circle on asphalt with chalk. Have one player stand in the center of the circle. This player may toss the ball into the air to himself or have a friend serve the balls from outside the circle. The player in the circle tries to receive the ball with his chest and drop it to his feet. If he can control the ball within the circle, award him a point. If not, he loses a point. Record his score after ten throws and have the players switch roles. Make the circle bigger if scoring points is too difficult, smaller if it's too easy.

The Matthews Move The most used and probably the most effective of all moves is the simple cut. A player is moving in one direction and suddenly moves off in another. The cut may be embellished with body feints to further throw opponents off balance. A slightly more advanced move that young players can master is called the Matthews move, after the legendary English star Sir Stanley Matthews, who relied on it to run by defenders during his thirty-three-year professional career.

What to Show Your Child

1. Dribble toward your opponent at half speed until you are about 2 yards away.
2. Then push the ball a few inches across your body with your right foot . . .
3. . . . while leaning your body left . . .
4. . . . at which point you slip your right foot around the ball so you can suddenly push it to the right.

5. Accelerate and run past your opponent.

6. To move to the left, reverse the directions in these steps.

Tips A move loses its effectiveness if it becomes predictable, so don't always cut in the same direction. Become comfortable cutting to both the right and left. Move around the defender's nondominant foot when possible. There will be less chance for the ball to be stolen.

Backyard Game Set two targets, such as trash cans or picnic table benches, 15 to 20 yards apart. Two players take turns using moves to try to pass each other and shoot at the target. Score one point each time a player uses a move successfully and one point if the target is hit.

Level III Skills

Level III skills may be focused upon with children ages eleven or older. They require more strength and coordination—and caution—than do Level I and Level II skills.

Push the ball across your body and lean in that direction.

Suddenly, push the ball in the opposite direction using the same foot . . .

. . . and accelerate past the defender.

Arch your back and keep your elbows and knees bent. Keep your eyes on ball, your chin tucked, and your neck stiffened.

Strike the ball with your forehead.

Heading Heading is a versatile skill that may be used to pass, shoot, receive, or clear the ball. Learning proper technique is key to preventing unnecessary discomfort, headaches, and jarring of the head.

What to Show Your Child

1. Facing the direction you want the ball to go . . .
2. . . . move to a position where the ball would land at your feet if you didn't head it.
3. Keep your eyes on the ball, chin tucked in, and neck muscles stiffened.
4. Arch your back, arms out, and keep your elbows and knees bent.
5. Strike the ball using your body, not your neck, to power the ball. With jump headers, try to strike the ball when you are at the peak of your jump.
6. Follow through, facing the target.

Use your body, not your neck, to power the ball, and follow through in the direction you want the ball to go.

Tips Do not teach heading until it becomes a part of your child's game—usually at age ten or older. Tell your child not to head the ball in situations when it would be better to receive it with the chest or foot. Be sure your child uses proper heading technique, using the entire body to help absorb the impact.

Backyard Game Timing is the key to successful heading. Here's a game that will help develop it: Make three 5-foot-wide goals spaced along an arc 4 or 5 feet apart. The player stands about 10 yards from the goals. Serve high balls from either end of the arc, about 15 or 20 yards away. The player must try to call out goal one, two, or three and then head the ball through the goal.

Although researchers generally agree that routine heading is not harmful, there's no sense in taking any unnecessary risks. In heading games, use a small, light ball such as a size 3 ball, a Nerf soccer ball, or a volleyball.

Pivot Turns Upon receiving the ball, a player should try to turn and face upfield, or face the nearest defender as quickly as possible. The pivot turn enables you to do this without wasting time. In no-pressure or low-pressure situations (the goalside defender is more than 10 yards away), pivot 180 degrees and face your defender. In medium-pressure situations, receive and pivot away from the defender.

Move to the pass and collect with the inside of the foot. Give and pivot.

Look up and decide how to play the ball next.

What to Show Your Child

1. Move to the oncoming ball when it's passed to you.
2. Stop a few feet from the ball and assume an open stance.
3. Reach for the ball with your receiving foot while balancing comfortably, knee bent, with the pivot leg.
4. Collect the ball with the inside of your foot . . .
5. . . . then give way after contact and pivot on your supporting foot.
6. The ball should end up just past you.

Tips Raise receiving foot to the height of the middle of the ball. Become comfortable pivoting either left or right.

Backyard Game With two players—one attacker and one defender—serve the ball on the ground to the attacker, who must turn to face the defender. The defender may approach to the left or right. Score one point for each time the attacker pivots in the correct direction.

Full Volley The full volley is usually taken as a shot and has the advantage of catching the keeper and defenders flat-footed. It is reserved for balls that are knee height or lower.

What to Show Your Child

1. Approach straight on or from a slight angle using small, quick steps.

With your kicking foot perpendicular to the ground . . .

. . . swing at the knee and strike the center of the ball. Make a short follow-through.

2. Plant your non-kicking foot a few inches to the side of the ball, toes pointed at your target.
3. Retract your kicking foot behind your body.
4. Swing forward at the knee and hip with the kicking foot perpendicular to the ground.
5. Hit the center of the ball with your instep.
6. Follow through straight forward, not up, with a short stroke.
7. You should land on your kicking foot well beyond where you made contact with the ball.

Tips The full volley is similar to striking an instep drive with two exceptions. The kicking leg must be raised slightly, and the follow-through should be short to keep the ball from going too high. Try to strike the ball when it is about a foot off the ground.

Backyard Game Mark a line with chalk about 30 inches high on a kick wall. Have players throw the ball high and well in front of themselves, or serve it to them from near the wall. Ask the players to run up and volley the served balls at the wall. Score two points for shots under the line and take away one point for shots over the line.

Half Volley A half volley is taken when a player doesn't have time to control the ball before shooting or clearing it from the goal area. It is similar to the full volley except that it is taken immediately after the ball has bounced.

What to Show Your Child
1. Run to a bouncing ball with quick, short steps.
2. Time your approach so you arrive when the ball is just about to bounce for the first or second time.
3. If possible, place your non-kicking foot to the side of where the ball will bounce.
4. Take a short backswing with your kicking foot.
5. Strike the ball with your instep just after it has hit the ground and started its bounce.
6. Swing from the hip and knee and strike the ball in the middle.
7. Land on your kicking foot.

Tips   To keep the ball from rocketing skyward, your follow-through should be short and low, parallel to the ground. Keep your toe pointed down throughout the kick.

Time your approach to reach the ball . . .

. . . so you may strike with your instep . . .

. . . just after it bounces.

Backyard Game Use the same game as described above for the full volley.

Juggling Many coaches will tell you that juggling the ball is not a valuable skill. I think they're wrong. While it's true you can play the game well without being able to juggle—just as you can play without being able to execute a bicycle kick—juggling will definitely give a player an edge. The ability to juggle, for example, enables a player to receive and tap a ball into the air before volleying a shot or clearance. Or, it may let a player reach back with her leg for a ball dropping behind her and flick it over her head and the head of a defender as she runs by her to collect the ball.

What to Show Your Child

1. To begin to learn to juggle, keep your foot level to the ground.
2. Make your ankle flexible but not loose.
3. Tap the ball at the start of your shoelaces.
4. Keep your eyes on the center of the ball and the ball close to your body.

5. Use a gentle flick of your foot to keep the ball bouncing to knee height.

Tips Remember that you command the ball—the ball doesn't command you. Stay relaxed and comfortable. Keep your toes straight to maintain a level surface with which to juggle. If you're having trouble juggling with your feet, try to get the juggling rhythm by using your thighs.

Backyard Game Children can play juggling games alone or with a group. The most basic game is to see how many times a player can juggle the ball without letting it touch the ground. You may also set up challenges, such as juggling with various parts of the body in sequence (foot to knee to head, and so on).

Juggling may be done with the foot, thigh, head, or other parts of the body.

The Stepover Move The stepover is one of several moves that involve stepping over the ball in order to fake in one direction, and then using the other foot to move the ball in the opposite direction.

What to Show Your Child

1. Dribble toward your opponent at half speed.
2. When you are about a yard or two away, move your right foot over and past the ball.
3. Lean your body right.
4. Plant your right foot.
5. Push the ball to the left with your left foot.
6. Accelerate and run past your opponent.
7. To cut to the right, reverse these directions and begin by moving your left foot over and past the ball.

Approach the defender at half speed. Step over the ball and lean one way.

Use your opposite foot to push the ball past the defender. Accelerate to full speed.

Tips The key to the success of most moves is to use two speeds, half and full. Typically, you approach an opponent at half speed. When the opponent leans the wrong way, you accelerate to full speed and pull away. Only you know when you're going to change gears and speed away. This gives you a split-second head start. Try to time your speed change for when your opponent has leaned the wrong way.

Backyard Game See "The Matthews Move" in the Level II Skills section earlier in this chapter.

Advanced Skills

There are soccer skills that are not recommended for young players. They include the side volley (striking a ball while it's a few feet off the ground), bicycle kick (striking a ball that is overhead), swerving kick (making a shot or pass so it curves to elude goalkeepers or defenders), and diving header (just what it sounds like).

Most of these should only be attempted by advanced players once they reach the age of thirteen or fourteen. They require strength, balance, and patience to learn. Swerved kicks put stress on the knees. Players who attempt bicycle kicks and diving headers must first learn to fall to the ground without injury. Teaching advanced skills before your child is able to execute them is frustrating and sometimes unsafe.

CHAPTER 6

Goalkeeping

Most very young children (ages six to nine) do not like to play in the goal during matches. They don't want the responsibility of stopping goals, afraid they will fail. A mistake anywhere else on the field is quickly forgotten or not even noticed. But in the goal area, a keeper's miskick or fumble is in the spotlight and can quickly result in a goal for the opposition.

Kids also shy away from playing goal because of the likelihood of getting hurt—either by a hard shot or by a charging opponent. For a young player, the position can be boring, especially when playing on a dominant team that allows few shots on goal. Most kids prefer to run around with everyone else, trying to score goals. For these reasons, goalkeepers are not used in matches by many recreation programs until kids reach third or fourth grade.

As kids get older, a few will become interested in the position. Sometimes it's the player who, not having success elsewhere on the field, settles upon the goal as a way to contribute. Other times it's a risk taker who is looking for a challenge and is willing to accept responsibility for single-handedly winning or losing the game.

Despite the fact that goalkeepers are not used in small-sided matches for young players, it's OK to begin teaching young kids goalkeeping skills in the backyard or at practice. In low- or no-pressure environments, most kids don't mind trying the position, and some will be curious, even enthusiastic, about learning goalkeeping skills. Those who have positive experiences with the position may step up to being keepers as they mature.

Even for kids who will never specialize in goalkeeping, learning to play the position is a good idea. By playing in the goal during training sessions, scrimmages, and occasionally in matches, a player gets a different perspective of the game. From the keeper's vantage point, you can see the entire field and begin to see tactics at work. You have time to observe the strengths and weaknesses of opponents. And there's no better way to learn how scoring opportunities develop than to stand in the shoes of a keeper. Finally, knowing how to play the goal gives players the option of switching to the position later in their careers.

Goalkeeping Skills

Unlike other positions, goalkeeping has its own set of skills. They fall into two basic categories: making saves and distributing the ball. *Making saves* includes knowing where to position yourself, how to stand in the ready stance, how to step to the ball, how to handle the ball when it gets to you (catch, punch, or parry), and how to protect yourself from injury. *Distributing* is what you do once you have made a save. It includes deciding when and from where to release the ball, to whom, and by what method (throw or kick).

Field skills are important for goalkeepers to have, as well. Rule changes in recent years have required keepers to become better at dribbling, receiving, and passing. No longer can they use their hands to scoop up a pass kicked from a teammate. They must play such balls with their feet—often in the face of pressure from opposing attackers. Keepers are also often responsible for taking goal kicks.

Finally, a keeper must be a good communicator. Keepers are often in the best position to call out information about what's happening on the field. For example, if a keeper knows she can be first to the ball, she should shout, "Keeper." If free to receive a pass from a pressured defender she yells, "Back." If it's clear that the defender cannot turn from pressure, the correct call is "Clear it!" In free-kick situations, keepers must quickly help position teammates in defensive walls to reduce the chance for a goal to be scored. Similarly, goalkeepers will organize the defenders in corner-kick situations, ensuring that both posts are covered and that all attackers are marked (covered).

Basic Goalkeeping Skills

Many parents and coaches pay little attention to teaching goalkeeping skills. This is partly due to the fact that many of the skills are similar to traditional American sports, such as catching a football or basketball. Nevertheless, players should be shown the proper techniques for catching a soccer ball.

Ready Stance A child who is not taught how to be ready for a shot will have a poor experience in goal. The ready stance allows the keeper to react quickly and to move in any direction in order to save a shot. The key is being loose and relaxed, not stiff and tense.

The ready stance allows you to react quickly to a shot from any direction.

What to Show Your Child

1. Raise your head but keep your neck muscles relaxed. Keep your eyes on the ball.
2. Hold your arms in front of your body with the elbows bent and the forearms parallel to the ground.
3. Raise your hands slightly above your elbows, palms down and extended forward.
4. Bend your body forward so that your shoulders are in front of your feet.
5. Bend your knees slightly and keep your feet even and slightly spread.

Tip Rest your weight on the balls of your feet, heels raised and toes pointing out.

Basic Contour Catch To catch a ball that is chest high or higher, use the contour catch. If you are unable to catch the ball cleanly, the hand positions shown in the photograph on the next page will enable you to block the ball effectively.

What to Show Your Child

1. Move so you are in front of the oncoming ball.
2. Raise your hands to catch the ball and . . .
3. . . . position them thumb to thumb.
4. Cup your hands so they are in the shape of the ball.

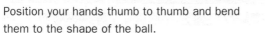
Position your hands thumb to thumb and bend them to the shape of the ball.

Catch the ball and bring it to your chest.

5. Flex your wrists forward and extend your arms slightly outward.
6. Catch the ball.
7. Bring it smoothly to your chest.

Tips Use two hands equally to make the catch. Once you've caught the ball, cover it with your hands and arms to keep from dropping it, especially when making a save in traffic.

Backyard Game Face off one player with a partner about 5 yards away. Have them take turns throwing the ball above chest height to each other. See how many catches they can make without dropping the ball. After every ten completions, each player takes a long step back. If players fail to make ten completions after several attempts, they must start over.

High Contour Catch The high contour catch is for balls that are played higher than you can reach without jumping. It's especially useful for catching crosses and corner kicks played across the box.

What to Show Your Child
1. Move quickly so you face the oncoming ball.
2. Raise your arms and leap from one foot.
3. Position your hands as for the basic contour catch.

Position your hands as for the basic contour catch.

Thrust one knee upward for extra lift and to protect yourself from onrushing attackers.

4. Make the catch and pull the ball to your body, protecting it with your hands and arms.

Tip Thrust one knee upward for extra lift and to protect yourself from onrushing attackers.

Backyard Game Same as for the basic contour catch, but the ball should be thrown so the players must jump to catch it. Start counting over if the ball is not thrown high enough.

Side Contour Catch The side contour catch is for balls shot to either side of you and so far out that you can't get in front of them.

What to Show Your Child
1. Move quickly to the ball.
2. Extend your arms to the path of the ball.

Extend your arms sideways to the path of the ball. Position your hands as for the contour catch, but place one hand behind the ball and one hand on top to prevent it from slipping through.

3. Position your hands thumb to thumb and cupped as for the basic contour catch.
4. Make the catch with one hand behind the top of the ball and the other behind the bottom of it.

Tips   When you attempt to save a ball while you are moving, there is a much greater chance of dropping it. Be prepared to fall on a dropped ball if necessary.

Backyard Game   Same as for the basic contour catch, but the ball should be thrown so players must move to the side to catch it. Alternate throwing from one side to the other side. Start counting over if the ball is not thrown wide enough.

Basket Catch   The basket catch is used for catching balls that come below chest height.

What to Show Your Child
1. Move quickly so you face the oncoming ball.
2. Lower your hands into the path of the ball, arms extended.
3. Position your hands little finger to little finger.
4. Bend at the waist as the ball reaches you and form a basket with your hands and arms.

Lower your hands into the path of the ball, arms extended, and position your hands little finger to little finger.

Bend at the waist as the ball reaches you and form a basket with your arms and hands.

Tip   After catching the ball, bend your upper body forward to cover the ball and lessen the chance of it rebounding into play.

Backyard Game   Same as for the basic contour catch, but the ball should be thrown below the player's waist. Start counting over if the ball is not thrown low enough.

Punting   Punt the ball when opponents cut off your ability to distribute to the flanks or when a long kick will give your defenders time to reorganize.

What to Show Your Child
1. Step in the direction you want to kick the ball.
2. If you're kicking right-footed, hold the ball in your left hand; if left-footed, hold it in your right hand.
3. Drop the ball and focus your eyes on the spot where you will kick it, slightly below its center.
4. Lock your ankle and point your toe away from your body.
5. Strike the ball with your instep.
6. Follow through high with your leg, but keep your head down.

Tip   For maximum distance, strike the ball just before it reaches the ground.

Backyard Game   Two partners take turns punting to each other. The first marks the spot of the first kick with a T-shirt. The second marks the spot where the first punt lands and punts from there. The second player needs to punt past the first one's starting spot to win a point. If the ball falls short, the point goes to the first punter. Continue in sets of ten. If it becomes obvious that one player is dominant, allow the weaker punter a handicap of several yards.

Parrying   The parry is one of the keeper's options when it looks impossible to catch the ball. Essentially it means to stop a hard shot with the heel or heels of your hands. You may choose to parry in any number of directions: down where you can pick it up, up and over the crossbar, up where you can catch it, or—in pressure situations—as wide as possible. Parrying is useful for young kids whose hands are often not large or strong enough to catch the ball.

What to Show Your Child
1. Reach toward the middle of the oncoming ball with the heel or heels of your hands.

2. Extend your arm or arms in the direction you want the ball to go.
3. If you want the parry to land near you, pull your hands back at contact to cushion the impact.
4. If you want the ball to travel some distance, stiffen your arm as the ball strikes the heel of your hand.

Tips Keep your fingers together to avoid sprains should you misjudge a parry. In high-pressure situations, where you must dive to make the save, try to parry the ball around the goalpost and out of play.

Backyard Game Two or more players parry the ball to each other and see how many times they can do it without the ball hitting the ground. Devise various challenges to make the game more interesting. For instance, try parrying while sitting on the ground or while moving.

Bowl Throw Use the bowl throw for short accurate passes.

What to Show Your Child
1. Hold the ball in front of you as you step in the direction you want to throw it.
2. Spread your fingers and cup the ball between your palm and forearm.
3. Bring the ball back, with your weight on your rear foot.
4. Swing in forward and release, bending your knees.
5. Smoothly "lay" the ball on the ground.

Spread your fingers and cup the ball between your palm and forearm.

Smoothly "lay" the ball on the ground. Point your front toes toward the target.

6. Follow through with your arm in the direction you want the ball to go.

Tips Point front-foot toes toward your target. Try to roll the ball so it does not bounce and is easy for your teammate to receive.

Backyard Game Set up several small goals, 24 inches wide and 10 to 15 yards apart. Place the goals as you would wickets for croquet. Find one or more partners and play soccer croquet using the bowl throw.

Sling Throw Use the sling throw to make accurate passes at medium distance.

What to Show Your Child
1. Stand parallel to the direction in which you want to throw the ball.
2. Hold the ball lightly between your palm and arm.
3. Bring back your throwing arm behind your body at waist height.
4. Balance on your back foot and arch your back.
5. Point your free arm in the direction you want to throw the ball.
6. Palm up, elbow locked, sling the ball over your head.
7. Step forward and shift your weight to your front foot.
8. Release the ball, using your body to add power to the throw.

Stand parallel to the direction you want to throw the ball and hold the ball lightly between your palm and arm.

Palm up, elbow locked, sling the ball over your head.

Prepare to catch the ball using the side contour catch.

Catch the ball away from your face to protect yourself from being kicked in the head.

Tips Point front-foot toes in the direction you want to throw. Release the ball at head height for maximum distance. By imparting a backspin to your throw, you can make the ball easier for your teammate to handle.

Backyard Game Set up a dozen cones and allow each player to use them as targets for his throws. Score one point each time he hits a cone. When playing with a partner, players should take turns retrieving the ball for each other.

Collapse Dive The collapse dive is for balls that you can't quite reach and still stay on your feet. Unlike the full extension dive, however, you're never completely airborne. Don't use the collapse dive if you can move in front of the ball and make the save without diving. By making saves look as easy as you can, you will build confidence in your teammates and demoralize your opponents.

What to Show Your Child
1. Stride forward to meet the shot, keeping both legs in contact with the ground.
2. Focus your eyes on the ball.
3. Catch the ball using the side contour catch (one hand behind and one on top of the ball).
4. "Place" the ball on the ground in front of you.

5. Fall to the ground, knees bent and legs raised slightly.
6. Pull the ball to your chest and roll away from danger to protect your head from being kicked after you've made the save.

Tips Use the ball to help cushion your landing. Try to control your fall to the ground. Do not flop or the ball will likely be jarred loose. Catch the ball away from your face, to protect yourself from being kicked in the head.

Backyard Game Have two players kneel facing each other, two or three yards apart. Instruct them to toss the ball back and forth, first to the left and then to the right. The receiving player catches the ball using the side contour catch and then collapses with the ball.

Sliding Save Use the sliding save to win balls that you can reach before the shooter can.

What to Show Your Child
1. Approach the ball hard with your body low.
2. Drop to your side and slide to the ball.
3. Extend your hands toward the ball, away from your face.
4. Position your body so it blocks as much of the goal as possible.
5. Catch the ball and pull it to your chest.

Reduce the angles from which the shooter can score by stepping forward to make saves. These photos show how the goal "shrinks" from the perspective of the shooter as the goalkeeper steps forward.

Tips Focus on the ball, not the striker. Upon making the catch, protect yourself by pulling your knees up and in toward your body.

Backyard Game Make two goals with cones about 20 yards apart. Two keepers stand in the goals and take turns dribbling toward each other and making sliding saves. Advise keepers to dribble at half speed to start. This will allow their partners to concentrate on sliding and hand positions when making the catch.

Reaction Save Use the reaction save to stop breakaways when you can't beat the shooter to the ball.

What to Show Your Child
1. Move out from the goal straight toward the ball.
2. Keep your eyes focused on the ball.
3. Remain standing to obscure as much of the goal as possible.
4. Lean slightly forward, hands down and palms out.
5. Make the catch using the appropriate hand positions, and the collapse dive if necessary.

Tips Be ready to react should the attacker decide to pass instead of shoot. If you are unable to catch the ball cleanly, be prepared to get up quickly and pick it up or to cover it.

Backyard Game Make two goals with cones about 20 yards apart. Two keepers stand in the goals and take turns dribbling toward each other and shooting from a range of about 5 yards. Vary the distance between goals and the size of the goals based on the age and skill of the keepers. Advise keepers to shoot at half speed to start. This will allow them to concentrate on diving and hand positions when making the catch.

Advanced Goalkeeping Skills

Teaching more advanced goalkeeping skills—drop kicks, tipping and punching the ball, extension dives, smother saves, building defensive walls, and handling penalty kicks and direct, indirect, and corner kicks—is beyond the capability of most parents and novice coaches. A child who is interested in learning more should be enrolled in goalkeeper camps. There, experts will teach skills, offer techniques that make goalkeeping safer, and discuss the psychology of the position.

Many clubs also organize clinics for goalkeepers, knowing that most coaches have little or no training in the position. They usually feature a goalkeeper coach from a nearby college. Sometimes the club will pay the fee and in other cases the parents do.

Specialized goalkeeper camps for kids are also available, usually as part of a general soccer camp. In these programs, goalkeepers train separately during part of the day and then have the opportunity to put their skills to the test during matches with field players. (For more on camps, see chapter 11.)

Goalkeeping Tactics

It's beyond the scope of this book to cover goalkeeping tactics in depth, but there are a few tactical questions that will come up as soon as most kids play the position: where to stand when you expect a shot, how far to come out, and where to play the ball once you've made the save.

Where to stand is largely determined by the position of the potential shooter. Reduce the angles from which an attacker may shoot the ball by moving toward the shooter. Doing so reduces the amount of goal open to a shooter as much as possible (see figure 6.1). Coming out also increases the pressure, often forcing the shooter to shoot before being ready.

How far to come out is also determined by several variables, including the number of attackers, the likelihood that the attacker with the ball will pass it, and how much defensive support the keeper has. Generally speaking, the more defenders, the closer the keeper stays to the goal. Few or no defenders forces a keeper to come well out into the

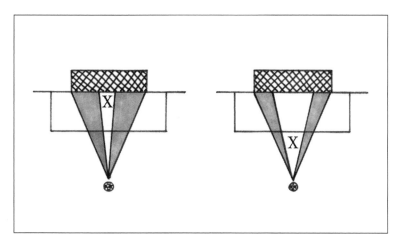

Figure 6.1: Moving toward the ball allows the goalkeeper to reduce the amount of goal open to the shooter.

penalty box or even beyond it to either win a ball or force the shot from as far from the goal as possible. A keeper must be careful, however, about coming out too far. Too much distance makes it easy for an at-tacker to dribble around the keeper or to chip it over the keeper's head for an easy goal. It's a delicate balance and takes lots of experience playing the position to make good judgments.

Where to play the ball, especially for young players, is relatively simple. The safest option is to throw or punt it to the flanks where teammates can play the ball forward. Teach keepers to avoid playing to the area in front of the goal where, if the ball is stolen, the opposition can easily score. And teach field players to be available for passes to the flanks.

CHAPTER 7

Mastering the Rules

The rules for soccer as we know it today were written in 1863 in England, and today's game is essentially the same as it was then. The object is for players to get the ball into the other team's goal more times than the other team puts it into theirs.

In addition to defining the object of the game and how goals are scored, rules are agreements as to what you can and can't do while playing the game. The agreement that sets soccer apart from most other sports is that the ball, once in play, cannot be advanced with the use of the hands except upon a throw-in or by the goalkeeper. Rules also define how players are able to keep the game moving through its natural pauses, such as when the ball is kicked out of play, when the keeper catches the ball, when a field player intentionally handles the ball, and so on.

Soccer is the easiest of all team sports to understand. A pregame coin toss determines which team will start with the ball. Play begins with a kickoff from the center circle on a field that is 110 to 120 yards long by 70 to 80 yards wide. All players start on their half of the field, and no one on the defensive team may enter the center circle until the ball has been touched.

Each team seeks to score by kicking the ball into the opponent's goal. A goal is scored only when the ball completely crosses the goal line between the goalposts. Two goals, one at each end of the field, measure 24 feet wide by 8 feet high. Directly in front of the goal is the goal area, 20 yards by 6 yards. Beyond the goal area is the 44-by-18-yard penalty area, which is marked to signify the only space where goalkeepers are

free to use their hands. The penalty spot is marked inside the penalty area. At all four corners are flags and a small arc marked just inside the field. Teams play ninety-minute games, which are divided into two forty-five-minute halves.

Teams consist of eleven players, who can be set up on the field in a variety of ways. Coaches, players, and teams are always looking to make tactical changes that will lead to success. Unlike players in most sports, soccer players don't necessarily have a specific position or area of the field that they need to cover. Team formations vary widely. A team may start a game with a 4-4-2 formation, but switch to a 4-2-4 late in the game if it's down a goal.

Top professional teams employ many formations, with each team hoping to unbalance the opposition's formation and create a weakness that can be exploited. This chess match of offense against defense takes place as play is evolving, without direct input from a coach. Unlike other sports, soccer has no time-outs or huddles and forces the players to think for themselves.

The goalkeeper plays in front of the goal and is the only player permitted to put a hand or arm on the ball. All other players use their feet, thighs, head, and other body parts to control the ball.

Attacking players can't get between the ball and the goal they are aiming for unless there are at least two defenders (one usually being the goalkeeper) between them and the goal line. If they do, they are offside. (For more on this, see "The Offside Rule" section later on page 97.)

A free kick is taken to restart play after an infraction or a score or if the ball has gone out of bounds over the goal line. There are two types of free kicks: A direct free kick can result in a goal without the ball having to be touched by another player on either team. An indirect free kick must first be touched by another player before a goal can be scored.

If the infraction occurs inside the penalty area, the innocent team receives a penalty kick. The ball is placed on a penalty spot 12 yards from the goal, and the defensive players must remain outside the area until the ball is kicked. The goalkeeper must remain on the goal line until the ball is kicked.

When the attacking team sends the ball completely over its opponent's goal line, a goal kick is taken by the defending team. The ball may be placed anywhere in the goal area and is not considered back in play until it has been kicked out of the penalty area.

When the defensive team sends the ball completely over its own goal line, a corner kick is taken by the attacking team. The ball is put back in play from the arc at the corner of the field. A goal may be scored directly from a corner kick.

If the ball goes completely over the touchline (sideline), the team that did not touch it last puts the ball into play with a throw-in. Throw-ins are taken from where the ball left the field and must be thrown with both hands while both feet are on the ground on or behind the touchline. A goal may not be scored directly off a throw-in. Throw-ins are the most frequent restarts; there could be more than fifty in a ninety-minute game.

Some games end in ties. Some go into sudden-death overtime, in which the first team to score (golden goal) wins. Some games that remain tied after overtime use a shootout to determine the winner. Each team takes five penalty kicks. The team scoring the most goals is the winner. If the game is still tied after five kicks per side, the shootout continues, with players from each team alternating shots until a winner is determined.

Playing by the Rules

Players, coaches, and teams are encouraged to play fair and in the spirit of the game. The referee, or ref, is in full control of a soccer match, enforcing the laws and stopping the game for any infringement. The ref has the final word, but may consult the assistant referees. The assistant referees help the referee with out-of-bounds calls and can signal fouls as well as offside.

Referees don't have it easy. They might run several miles in a game, and they must be aware of twenty-two players and the ball at all times. The ref must determine the type of foul and its penalty—all in a split second.

Basically, there are three categories of offenses. *Minor offenses* result in indirect free kicks. *Major offenses* result in direct free kicks. *Misconduct* results in a yellow or red card.

Players—and parents—need to understand these offenses, accept the ref's decisions without argument, and show good sportsmanship.

Free Kicks

Soccer is a physical sport. Breaking a rule is called a foul and is penalized by a free kick for the team that was fouled. A free kick gives the innocent team a chance to score.

A *direct free kick* is awarded for fouls that involve physical contact or a hand ball (that is, touching the ball with any part of the arm or hand). When a direct free kick occurs, the fouled team is awarded a free kick from the point of the foul. A direct free kick can result in a goal without the ball having to be touched by another player on either team.

If a direct-kick foul occurs in the penalty area, the direct kick becomes a penalty kick. The ball is placed on a spot 12 yards from the center of the goal, and any player on the offensive team may shoot at the goal. The goalkeeper may move on the goal line before the kick. If the shot does not go in but stays in play, the kicker may touch the ball only after it has been touched by another player on either team.

An *indirect free kick* is awarded for all other fouls, including offside. An indirect free kick is taken from the point of the foul. An indirect free kick must first be touched by another player before a goal can be scored. An indirect kick awarded in the penalty area is played like any other indirect kick.

Teams often defend against free kicks by setting up a "wall" to block the kick. A wall may consist of any number of players lined up shoulder to shoulder. The closer the free kick is taken to the goal, the more players in the wall; there are usually around five players in a wall. These players must stay at least 10 yards from the ball and may not move until the ball is kicked. A player from the offensive team is permitted to create an opening in the wall by standing in it and moving away when the ball is kicked, but may not push a defender out of place while doing so.

Minor Offenses

Minor offenses, which are penalized by an indirect free kick, are as follows:

1. Dangerous play—playing in a manner that could result in injury to the player or to any other player. Examples include attempting to kick the ball while the keeper is holding it or attempting to kick a ball close to the head of an opponent.
2. Impeding the progress of an opponent—blocking an opponent's path while not attempting to play the ball.
3. Preventing the goalkeeper from letting go of the ball.

4. Releasing the ball and then putting a hand on it again before it has been touched by another player.
5. Holding the ball for longer than six seconds after gaining possession.
6. Using the hands to control a ball that has been received from a deliberate kick by a teammate.
7. Using the hands to control a ball that has been directly received from a throw-in taken by a teammate.
8. Wasting time—using tactics to hold up the game.

(**Note:** The last five offenses must be committed by goalkeepers in their team's own penalty area.)

Major Offenses

Major—or penal—offenses, which are penalized by a direct free kick, are as follows:

1. Kicking or attempting to kick an opponent.
2. Tripping or attempting to trip an opponent; this includes using the legs or stooping in front of (or behind) an opponent.
3. Jumping at an opponent.
4. Charging from behind or in a violent or dangerous manner (unless the opponent is guilty of obstruction).
5. Striking or attempting to strike an opponent; this includes a goalkeeper's throwing the ball at an opponent.
6. Pushing an opponent.
7. Spitting at an opponent.
8. Holding an opponent with the hand or arm.
9. Deliberately touching the ball with any part of the hand or arm (except for the defending goalkeeper in the penalty area).
10. Making contact with the opponent before touching the ball when tackling.

(**Note:** The first six offenses result in a direct free kick if, in the referee's judgment, they were committed carelessly, recklessly, or with excessive force.)

Cautions and Ejections

The referee has the power to punish minor and major offenses further if they are considered serious enough. In cases of blatant or repeated

fouls, the ref may issue a yellow card (a caution) to one or more players. Anyone receiving two yellow cards in one match is sent off the field; the ejected player's team plays short-handed for the remainder of the game. For even more serious fouls, the referee can immediately issue a red card, ejecting a player from the game.

A referee may warn a player to shape up before a yellow card is issued, but more serious acts (swearing, spitting at an opponent, and so on) will not be tolerated and will result in a player being sent off the field at once.

The yellow and red card system was developed because players and coaches who didn't speak the same language as the referee weren't always certain they had been cautioned. Referee Ken Aston was driving home after working a game more than thirty years ago and was inspired by the colors of a traffic light. Colored lights, he surmised, could be used to get beyond the language barrier that was often faced in international matches. Yellow and red cards were born!

Players will be cautioned and shown the *yellow card* if they commit any of the following offenses:

1. Using unsporting behavior; this includes pushing, deliberately handling the ball, faking an injury, and preventing the goalkeeper from releasing the ball.
2. Showing dissent by word or action; arguing with the referee, including (for a goalkeeper) leaving the penalty area to engage the ref in a debate.
3. Persistently infringing the Laws of the Game; this includes repeatedly committing fouls and failing to restart play properly after being warned.
4. Delaying the restart of play; this includes kicking or throwing the ball away to prevent a free-kick restart, throw-in, or corner kick and excessively celebrating a goal.
5. Failing to respect the required distance on a free kick or corner kick; players must be at least 10 yards away.
6. Entering or reentering the field without the referee's permission.
7. Deliberately leaving the field without the referee's permission.

Players will be shown the *red card* and sent off if they commit any of the following offenses:

1. Serious foul play.
2. Violent conduct.
3. Spitting at an opponent or any other person.
4. Denying an opponent a goal or an obvious goal-scoring opportunity by deliberately handling the ball.
5. Denying an obvious goal-scoring opportunity by an offense punishable by a free kick or a penalty kick.
6. Using offensive, insulting, or abusive language.
7. Receiving a second caution (yellow card) in the same match.

Commonly Misunderstood Calls

Everyone involved in the sport of soccer needs a good knowledge of the Laws of the Game. Knowing and understanding the rules will help you to better enjoy the game. Here's a quick look at five of the game's often-misunderstood calls.

Advantage Just because you spot a foul at your child's next game that the referee has seemingly overlooked, don't feel the need to blurt out, "Hey, ref, you missed a foul!" Chances are, the ref saw it and is just applying the advantage rule.

The referee retains the option of ignoring a foul. If the ref believes that the team that was fouled would lose an advantage—a quick counter-attack or a good shot on goal—the referee may extend both arms forward and shout, "Play on!" This lets everyone know that the ref is aware of the foul but thinks that stopping play would benefit the team that committed the foul more than the team that was fouled. The advantage rule is usually applied in the attacking third of the field when the fouled team retains possession of the ball or would lose a potential goal-scoring opportunity. The referee is ignoring the whistle for the good of the game. After a few seconds, the ref can decide to stop play and award a free kick if an advantage does not materialize.

The advantage should be evident, clear, and immediate. The offended player or team must have clear possession and the clear advantage that they had before the infraction. When in doubt, the referee shouldn't apply this rule.

Advantage is applied less often at the youth level. The referee generally calls the foul so young players are taught that all fouls are unfair.

Charging Many referees incorrectly penalize a fair charge. The thing to consider when two players make body contact is whether or not they were both playing the ball. If a big guy and a little guy go after the ball, the smaller one may very well end up on the ground. That is not necessarily a foul.

If a player looks at the opponent just prior to charging in, then it is very likely going to be a foul charge. When judging the charge, referees must read intent in the eyes and face and look for non-shoulder contact. A fair charge doesn't have to be weak. It can be hard, but it can't be violent.

Hand Ball No player other than a goalkeeper in the penalty area is allowed to touch the ball with any part of the arm, from the shoulders to the fingertips. But touching the ball with your hands is not necessarily a foul.

The referee must judge whether the hand ball was committed on purpose. A nondeliberate hand ball is not a foul. To fall and accidentally touch the ball is not a foul. A hand ball must be deliberate. A hand ball is deliberate when a player extends an arm to present a larger target or moves the hands toward the ball. Instinctive movements of the hands or arms to protect against being hit in the face, groin, or breast are not considered deliberate handling of the ball.

Female players are permitted to protect their chests with crossed arms. When they do this, they can't move their hands and they have to keep their arms pressed close to their chest. They are not permitted to lift their arms or to redirect the ball with their arms or hands in any way. A ref who believes a player has moved her arms or hands may call a foul.

If a hand ball by a defensive player goes into the defended goal, the score counts because of the aforementioned advantage rule.

Obstruction Obstruction is not allowing an opponent a clear shot at playing a ball while not in possession of the ball. Obstruction is fair when the ball is within playing distance (usually on the ground and about three feet away). Unfair obstruction is the often deliberate action of one player that impedes the progress of an opponent; for example, a player with or without the ball who backs into an opponent is guilty of obstruction. On the other hand, a defender who is caught off-balance by a quick, clever move by an opponent may be unable to react. The ensuing collision is often wrongly called obstruction, whereas the correct call is unfair charging.

A player can legally obstruct if the ball is rolling out of bounds.

Slide Tackling or Tripping A player slide tackles when he drops and slides on the ground in an attempt to win the ball or knock it away from an opponent. If, in the referee's judgment, the player is not attempting to play the ball, a direct free kick is awarded to the opposing team. A careless or reckless slide tackle may result in a yellow card. If the ball is played first, however, no foul should be called—even if the slide tackle is followed by an unintentional trip.

Players often dive to create a foul. Diving is simply an act by a player to invoke the awarding of a free kick or a penalty kick by the referee. It is usually a desperate measure made by a player about to lose control of the ball. A player who sees a scoring opportunity slipping away is apt to be tempted to dive. Referees should be aware of this and should caution players for unsporting behavior.

The Offside Rule The offside rule is the least understood and most controversial of them all. Even the top professionals are at times unsure if they are offside or not.

Designed to prevent attacking players from hanging out by the opposing goal and waiting for easy chances to score, the law states that players are in an offside position if they are closer to their opponents' goal line than the ball, unless they are in their own half of the field or are not closer to the goal than two opponents (including the goalkeeper) at the instant the ball is played. A player who is level (even) with the opponents is not in an offside position. To be called offside, the player must also interfere with play or with an opponent, or try to gain an advantage by being in an offside position.

Makes perfect sense, right?

What's important to understand is that a player's position when receiving the ball doesn't matter. What does matter is the position when the ball is actually played forward. A referee won't whistle an offside infraction until the ball is passed or shot. If, at the moment the

Figure 7.1: The highlighted attacker is not violating the offside rule in the first diagram, but is in an offside position in the second.

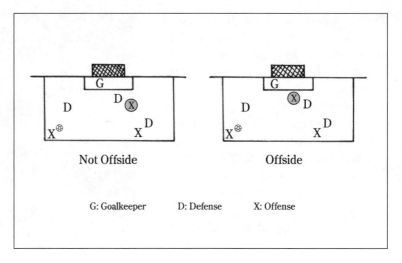

Not Offside   Offside

G: Goalkeeper   D: Defense   X: Offense

ball is passed, there are fewer than two defenders (counting the goal-keeper) between an offensive player and the goal, the offensive player is offside—but being level with the last defender other than the goal-keeper is OK and the player is not offside.

Spectators sometimes yell for an offside call when they see an opposing forward get a pass behind their team's defense. But they must be aware of the player's original position. Because a player even with or in front of a defender when the ball is kicked—and thus onside—may outrun the defender, the player may appear offside when receiving the pass. If the player was onside when the ball was first played forward, there is no offside.

Making matters even more complicated is the fact that it is not an offense to be in an offside position. Is the player in the offside position interfering with the play or gaining an advantage by being in this position? A player who is in an offside position but who has no chance of reaching the ball before anyone else is not interfering with the play and should not be penalized for being offside. Offside should only be called if the offside player interferes with or distracts a defender. A player who is standing in front of the goalkeeper, for example, may affect the keeper's line of vision and concentration. The keeper may have to allow for the offside player's presence.

The referees must take a number of things into account when determining whether a player was interfering or gaining an advantage by being in an offside position. Was the player moving toward or away from the goal? How did the other players react to his presence? Had the player been hanging out near the goal and waiting for a "garbage" goal? Was the player injured? The answers to these questions will help the referee make the correct call.

Making the correct call becomes even trickier after a shot is made and it bounces off a post, crossbar, or keeper to another attacker. The original shooter might suddenly wind up in an offside position. If the second attacker shoots and scores at this moment, the goal might be negated with an offside call. It would depend on whether the referee felt that the first shooter's proximity to the keeper had affected the play.

Players cannot be in an offside position during a goal kick, a throw-in, or a corner kick.

Following an offside call, the opposing team restarts with an indirect free kick. This is taken from the spot where the foul occurred, unless the infringement is committed in the opponent's goal area. In this case, the free kick is taken from any point within the goal area.

An offside trap is a tactic used by defenders to force offensive players deliberately offside. While marking the offensive players, the defenders suddenly move away from the goal as the ball is about to be played, leaving the offensive players in an offside position. This is a tough tactic to master, but if used properly, it is an effective method of frustrating attacks.

If the offside rule is still a bit confusing to you, just imagine how difficult it is for a referee to call during a fast-moving game!

Rule Variations for Youth Leagues

The game that has been discussed so far in this chapter is the standard outdoor game. For younger players, however, rules are often adjusted. The game changes as kids age, but the object remains the same!

- **Equipment:** Not all players need high-tech cleats with replaceable studs or other fancy gadgets. In many organizations, including the USYSA, sneakers are OK for very young players.
- **Goals:** Most professional goalkeepers are 6 feet tall—or taller. Most kids aren't. For that reason, many youth organizations allow smaller goals. In AYSO, for instance, it's up to each particular region to determine what goal size to use.
- **Substitutions:** At high levels, only a certain number of substitutions are allowed, and a player who has left a match cannot return. The FIFA standard is three subs per game. Youth leagues are often more flexible. Many have no limits on subs and allow for unlimited reentries.

- **Balls:** The pros use a size 5 ball, which is 27–28 inches in circumference and weighs 14–16 ounces. A size 5 ball may be too big for small children to handle, so many people recommend that children under the age of eight use a size 3 ball (23–24 inches, 8–10 ounces). Children eight to twelve should use a size 4 ball (25–26 inches, 11–13 ounces), and children thirteen and over should use a size 5 ball.

- **Game length:** The standard outdoor game is ninety minutes with a fifteen-minute halftime. Youth leagues use shorter games, often broken into halves (or even quarters) with a five- to ten-minute halftime. The following game lengths are good standards to go by: U-8, forty minutes; U-10, fifty minutes; U-12, sixty minutes; U-14, seventy minutes; U-16, eighty minutes; U-19, ninety minutes.

- **Fields:** Kids can fatigue quickly playing on a regulation field. USYSA recommends 20 x 30 (yards) for U-6, 30 x 50 for U-8, 50 x 70 for U-10, and 100 x 50 up to 120 x 80 for U-11 and up.

- **Small-sided:** Small-sided soccer (using fewer than eleven players per side) is the preferred way to bring youngsters into the sport. It allows for greater exposure to the ball (more touches) and increased skill development. AYSO strongly encourages small-sided games in younger divisions and permits such games for all divisions. In the USYSA, U-6 teams play 3v3, U-8 teams play 4v4, U-10 teams play 8v8, and teams U-11 and older play 11v11.

- **Miscellaneous:** The variations that can be made to the standard game are endless. Some leagues don't use keepers. Others don't apply the offside rule. Penalty kicks aren't allowed in some leagues. Often, a score isn't recorded. Any changes should be made with the players' interest in mind. Fun is the top priority.

Changes to the Laws of the Game

The International Football Association Board holds an annual meeting where it debates and decides upon changes in the Laws of the Game. The International F.A. Board has eight members, and it takes six affirmative votes for a change to be accepted. Some not-so-old rule changes are listed in this section.

A 1992 rule change prohibited goalkeepers from handling balls received via a kick from a teammate. This rule was implemented to stop delaying tactics, make the goalkeeper a more active field player, and increase scoring. (To get around this rule, a player may attempt to

AYSO Recommendations for Different Age Groups

Age Group	Field Size	Players Per Team	Ball Size	Game Length	Misc.
U-6	25 x 20	3	3	32	no keepers
U-8	50 x 30	4	3	40	no keepers
U-10	70 x 50	8	4	50	keepers optional
U-12	100 x 50	11	4	60	
U-14	100 x 50	11	5	70	
U-16	100 x 50	11	5	80	
U-18	100 x 50	11	5	90	

stop the ball, lift it with a foot, and then head it back to the keeper. This is considered unsporting behavior and earns the player a yellow card.)

In 1996, linesmen were renamed referee's assistants because their role had become more important and also in recognition of the fact that more females held this position.

In 1997, it was ruled that a goal may be scored directly from the kickoff and directly from a goal kick. Also, the phrase "without moving his feet" was deleted from Law 14: The Penalty Kick. This meant that goalkeepers could move side-to-side along their own goal line during a penalty kick.

According to a 2000 rule change, the goalkeeper now has six seconds to put the ball back into play after taking control of it with the hands and can take an unlimited number of steps in that time. Under the old rule, the keeper had five to six seconds to release the ball and was not allowed to take more than four steps while holding the ball. The intent of the new rule is to make the game a little faster and a little more exciting to watch.

SAY has already reacted to this new rule change. "We must remember that SAY is a recreational program and that a period of seven or eight seconds is 'no big deal,'" says Commissioner Roland Bedard. "The spirit of this rule is to prohibit delaying tactics and have the ball back in play as soon as possible. That is what the referees are to watch for." This rule will apply to SAY teams at the U-12 through U-19 age levels. Players under ten will play under the unlimited time and steps rule, as long as clearing is done without delay.

CHAPTER 8

Buying Soccer Equipment

A nice thing about soccer is that it requires very little equipment to play. The equipment required is very simple: supportive shoes, shin guards, and a T-shirt, socks, and shorts—and a ball. That said, we live in America, where tens of thousands of people spend their workdays dreaming up ways to make us believe we need more than we do—more bells and whistles, more performance, the latest technological advances in materials, and so on. So it is with soccer. There are shoes with rubber scales on the outer surface to help players make better contact with the ball and to give their shots more power. There are balls that fly truer and with more power. There are uniform fabrics that wick moisture from your skin to keep you drier and more comfortable. There are even shin guards enhanced with Kevlar and titanium, marketing ploys aimed at making you believe these products will help protect your child's legs from injury.

Some of it is, of course, hogwash. Big marketing companies come up with new twists and star endorsements every year or so in an effort to get your kids excited about buying their products—and to get you to open your wallet wider.

Unless you feel a huge need to support the incentive plans of the marketing departments of big corporations, or feel obligated to indulge your child's every whim, keep the words "simple," "good quality," and "right size" in your mind every time you walk through the doors of a soccer retailer or sports shop. And remember that many of the greatest players ever to grace a soccer field began playing without shoes, shin guards, or uniforms, and with a ball made of tightly wound rags and stockings.

Buying Balls

During my high school playing days, soccer balls were made of leather. They were quite beautiful when new, but after a bit of use—especially in foul weather and on abrasive surfaces—they became heavy, hard, and rough around the seams.

Today's balls are either made of PVC (a relatively hard, tough plastic sheet) or with softer, pliable polyurethane sheets. Balls made with PVC are called molded balls because the panels are glued and pressed to a core. They are low cost but also hard and don't have a lot of bounce. Sold in toy stores, molded balls are all too often what a child gets first.

Polyurethane balls feel and bounce better than molded balls and are easier to control. They are made by stitching twelve pentagon-shaped panels and twenty hexagon-shaped panels together and inserting a bladder. Other hand-stitched ball designs are made with six or eighteen panels.

Not all polyurethane balls, however, are created equal. The thicker the outer polyurethane layer and the more layers in the backing or lining under the polyurethane cover, the better (and more expensive) the ball. Balls with four layers of lining hold their shape, feel softer, and give better touch (control) than balls with two layers. A foam layer may also be used as a backing to improve softness. To find out about the construction of the ball you're buying, ask the retailer or check the listing in the manufacturer's catalog that most soccer retailers have on file in their stores.

Bladders Make a Difference, Too The bladder is like a heavy-duty balloon inside the ball. The bladder's valve, a small rubber tube, lets air in when you insert a pump needle, but not out once the needle is removed.

The bladders of most top-of-the-line balls are made of natural latex rubber. These bladders are popular because they're soft and elastic, giving players better control over the ball. Carbon latex bladders are extremely soft and cost a little more. Unfortunately, all latex bladders are

What Size Ball Is Right for Your Child?	
Use a size	*For a child aged*
3	5 to 7
4	8 to 11
5	12 to adult

Be sure to choose the correct size of soccer ball for your child. The right size ball has a big effect on a child's ability to execute successful passes.

relatively permeable and lose air quickly. They need to be pumped up every few days to be at the correct pressure for playing. Balls should be inflated until they can be compressed only slightly when squeezed from opposite sides.

Bladders made with synthetic (butyl) rubber or polyurethane retain air for several months, but they are harder and less elastic than latex bladders—especially in cold weather. Butyl or polyurethane bladders don't bounce as well or go as far when kicked as balls with latex bladders. New formulations of butyl such as "high-rebound" butyl, however, are nearly as soft as latex. Bladders made of this material will retain air for several weeks.

Ball Buyer's Checklist

- **Size:** Balls come in sizes that should be clearly marked on the ball. Use the chart above to determine the size recommended by the U.S. Youth Soccer Association for your child. A size 3 ball should measure 23 to 24 inches in circumference (the widest distance around a sphere); size 4 is 25 to 26 inches; and size 5 is 27 to 28 inches.
- **Weight:** A size 5 ball should not weigh more than 16 ounces nor less than 14 ounces, according to FIFA. There are no weight guidelines for smaller balls. Several manufacturers, including Nike, Adidas, and Kwik Goal, have marketed a size 5 ball at the

Look for FIFA Marks

A ball may be kicked as many as 2,000 times in an average game, so it's important that every ball meet a certain set of standards. Many balls include inscriptions signaling official authority or approval, but these are often meaningless. FIFA, soccer's world governing body, has set up a quality control program that puts balls through laboratory tests simulating game action. Two marks—FIFA INSPECTED and FIFA APPROVED—are used on balls that have passed the tests done at the Swiss National Research Laboratories. More than fifty manufacturers have qualified to bear the FIFA marks on the balls they make.

A ball is designated as "FIFA Inspected" after it passes the following six tests:

Circumference: The circumference must be the same all around the ball so it will move predictably. The diameter of the ball is measured at ten points and the mean average is calculated.

Roundness: The ball must not have any uneven seams that can change its shape. The diameter of the ball is measured at sixteen points and the mean average is calculated. The difference between the highest and lowest diameter must be no more than a predetermined percentage of the mean diameter.

Rebound: Balls must bounce between certain predetermined heights. The ball is dropped ten times onto a steel panel from a height of 2 meters.

Weight: The ball is weighed three times in a sealed cabinet to make sure it meets the predetermined specifications.

Water Absorption: The ball is turned and squeezed 250 times in a tank of water to make sure it isn't absorbing too much water.

Loss of Pressure: The ball is inflated to a certain pressure and checked seventy-two hours later to make sure it hasn't lost more than a predetermined amount of air.

A ball is designated as "FIFA Approved" after it has passed the above six tests at a higher level and has undergone a seventh test:

Shape and Size Retention: The ball is fired 2,000 times against a steel plate at 35 miles per hour. The seams and air valves must be undamaged, and the loss of pressure must be minimal.

low end of the weight range in efforts to improve ball performance and to reduce the impact of heading.

- **Circumference:** Use a tape measure to find a ball's circumference. Choose a ball that's closer to the minimum rather than the maximum circumference, because balls have a way of expanding with use and repeated inflations.

- **Ball construction:** Choose a hand-sewn ball with a polyurethane cover and a natural latex, carbon latex, or high-rebound butyl bladder. Check to see that the stitching is tight and regular. Keep a molded ball on hand if your child plays on abrasive surfaces, such as asphalt or concrete.
- **Cost:** Balls range in price from $6 to $160, but parents and coaches of recreation and travel team players can buy perfectly acceptable balls in the $15 to $60 price range. For backyard training balls, spend at the lower end of the range. If you're a coach buying match balls, spend at the middle or higher end of the range.

Buying Shoes

In soccer, feet do most of the work. It follows that shoes are a player's most important piece of soccer equipment. They offer your child's feet support and stability for running, protection for getting kicked or stepped on, and a stable surface with which to touch, receive, and kick the ball.

Your child's first shoe can be a sneaker. It's fine for kicking the ball around in the backyard or at a nearby park. Just be sure the sneakers have low, firm outer soles—called *outsoles* to differentiate them from insoles or linings—for stability. Thick or high outsoles like the ones on running shoes and fashion sneakers can cause twisted ankles or tripping.

Types of Soccer Shoes There are four basic types of outsoles on soccer shoes, each designed for different playing surfaces or field conditions: turf, firm ground, soft ground, and flat. The easiest way to tell what playing condition a shoe is designed for is to count the studs. The more studs, the more evenly a player's weight is distributed and the better-suited the shoe is for playing on hard ground.

If your child usually plays on artificial surfaces or fields where the soil is compacted because of lack of water or overuse of the field, consider a *turf (TF)* shoe as your primary shoe. They're equipped with dozens of small rubber studs on the outsole that offer good traction and absorb shock that can cause stress to your feet. Turf shoes typically have more cushioning built into the heel than do soft ground shoes. Uppers can be synthetic or leather.

Firm ground (FG) outsoles typically have twelve medium-length studs or blades. This type is considered as close as you can get to an all-purpose shoe and can be used on soft and hard ground. Many models have outsoles made of polyurethanes with two densities—hard

Figure 8.1: The parts of a soccer shoe.

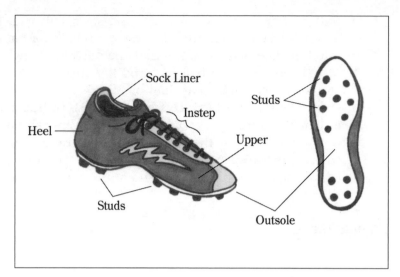

at the tip for durability and soft at the sole and stud base to provide a little give and cause less stress on the foot. Some have outsoles made of rubber, which is even less stressful to the feet.

Both Nike and Adidas make firm ground shoes specifically for women. The last (frame) upon which the shoe is built is narrow, which some female players prefer.

If your child is fourteen years old or older and plays often on soft ground, consider a *soft ground (SG)* shoe with replaceable studs or with a bladed outsole designed for soft conditions. The studs and blades of soft ground shoes are longer, and there are typically only six to ten per shoe. Fewer studs or blades help prevent mud from clinging to the bottom of your shoes. Most players do not need replaceable-stud shoes until they reach high school age.

Flats or indoor shoes are similar to sneakers (no studs), but may have soccer-shoe uppers. The outsoles are typically made of gum rubber and have more cushioning than found in shoes with studs. If your child plays indoors in warm conditions where heat builds up in the shoes, the ability of the shoe to breathe or vent is important. Otherwise, players may end up with big blisters on the undersides of their feet. Leather or suede shoes have the edge over synthetic materials, such as microfibers, when it comes to breathability.

What Is the Best Shoe Choice for Your Child? Age, playing surface, field conditions, skill level, playing style, position, foot shape, and appearance can all affect which shoe to buy for your child. The decision, especially if your child already has a favorite brand, can be daunting. There are, however, several ways to judge shoes:

Weight Lightweight shoes allow kids to run faster and tire less than heavy ones. The very lightest shoe, however, may not be the best choice. Many players, especially defenders, prefer a slightly heavier shoe because it offers more protection, foot support, and stability.

If you expect your child to often play in wet conditions, you may want to consider a shoe made with a synthetic, or microfiber, upper. Microfibers are lighter than leather when both are dry—and leather gets even heavier in wet conditions. Kangaroo leather, for example, can absorb more than 100 percent of its weight in water, whereas microfiber uppers absorb very little and remain much lighter.

Fit When it comes to choosing a shoe, comfort is key. That means soft uppers, good support, and cushioning—and the right fit. Don't be afraid to have your child try on every pair in the store in order to find the pair that feels best. Keep in mind that a size 8 from one manufacturer may be equal to a half size more or less from a different maker.

Leather shoes are more forgiving when it comes to fit than synthetics because they will stretch slightly to accommodate the shape of the foot. Kangaroo leather stretches more than cowhide. Synthetic uppers, including microfibers, do not stretch. If the fit is not right to begin with, it's not going to get better as the shoe breaks in— and your child may suffer with chafing and blisters.

Try on both shoes. One foot may be slightly bigger than the other. There should be no more than ⅜ inch between the tip of the big toe and the front of the shoe (less, once your child's foot growth slows down). Check the row of eyelets (small holes for receiving a shoestring) when you lace up the shoes. If the rows are parallel, the shoe is the right width. If the eyelets are wider apart at the top than the bot-

tom, the shoe may be too narrow. If the eyelet rows narrow at the top, or if they look too close together, the shoe may be too wide.

Avoid the temptation to buy oversize shoes or to continue to use shoes your child has outgrown. You may get an extra season of use by making your child wear ill-fitting shoes, but they may ruin the fun of playing, as well as cause pain, blisters, and other foot problems. Reduce shoe-buying costs by organizing a shoe swap with the other teams in your club. Other good sources for serviceable shoes include checking with parents of older players and visiting garage sales in neighborhoods with soccer-age kids.

Touch When your child tries on a pair of shoes, borrow a ball from the salesperson. Ask your child to drop it and try some foot catches. Is the shoe upper soft enough so that the ball can be felt as it touches the instep (the broad laced area) and toes? Now have the child push the ball along the floor. Does the feeling come through well enough to guide the ball without looking at where it is touching the shoe? The ability to feel the ball is important for many skills, including dribbling and receiving.

Many of the elite players I've spoken to prefer to have as little as possible between their foot and the ball. That's why thin and supple kangaroo leather has become such a popular material for uppers. It's also why some designers have shifted the laces to the side of the shoe. In theory, having fewer layers of material (tongue, laces, eyelets, leather, and liners) on the instep helps the player feel the ball better.

Cost If your budget is limited—and even if it isn't, and you don't like to spend money unnecessarily—your best strategy may be to select good but moderately priced shoes for each of the categories your child is likely to need. For the price of one pair of high-performance shoes, you can buy three pairs of shoes and be ready for every condition: indoor, turf or hard ground, and soft ground. If you can afford only one pair of outdoor shoes, buy firm ground shoes.

Be Realistic About Shoes No shoe, even one that's loaded with high-tech features, is going to make your child a great player. That's going to take practice, training, intelligence, and effort. If your child is nine or ten years old, you don't need fancy or specialized shoes. It's unlikely that friction patches on shoes will enable your youngster to swerve that next corner kick (kids that age are not strong enough yet), and soft ground shoes are for people so big that their weight makes it difficult to stop, start, and change direction in soft conditions.

Caring for Shoes

When I received my first good baseball mitt, my dad introduced me to the rituals of leather care. I was taught to regularly rub glove oil into my mitt and to store it with a ball in the pocket so the glove would keep its shape. Leather soccer shoes should receive the same sort of reverential treatment.

Show your child how to clean their shoes after each match—or at least once a week. Use a wet sponge to wipe off mud and an old toothbrush to remove dirt in the seams and creases. Many children can handle this chore, so try to get your child involved in cleat care. Once they're clean, rub leather conditioner into the shoe uppers. If you are going to have your child do this, look for a conditioner without petroleum distillates; they're safer and just as effective. Avoid using wax-based products, which seal the leather, preventing it from breathing. This results in sweaty, uncomfortable feet—and odors.

Note: Leather conditioners will not prevent your child's shoes and feet from becoming wet when playing on a wet field or in the rain. Nothing will, given the low cut of most soccer shoes.

After the game or practice, advise your child to wipe the mud from the cleats and to stuff them with newspaper. The newspaper, much like the ball I used in my Little League days, helps the shoes keep their shape. It also soaks up some of the moisture. Allow shoes to dry at room temperature; do not apply additional heat, or the leather may become stiff and the shoes uncomfortable.

If your child is eleven or twelve and plays on a recreation team, buy a pair of turf shoes. They're good in most conditions and won't stress growing feet.

If your child is prone to aches and pains in the feet and legs, consider shoes with a turf-style or rubber-molded outsole. They're heavier than shoes with a polyurethane outsole, but because rubber gives a little, they are more comfortable and less stressful on joints while your child is in the peak growth years.

If your child is the type who tosses shoes into the garage between practices, don't invest in shoes with expensive leather uppers. Until players are willing to clean and condition their own shoes regularly, a shoe with a low-maintenance synthetic upper is the best choice.

If your child is fourteen or fifteen, has a masterful touch, and plans to try out for the ODP team, then you may consider buying a top-of-the-line shoe with the features that sound good to you. If nothing else, owning the best possible shoes may give your child the psychological boost needed to make the team. And if the shoe designers have done their jobs right, the shoes may give a real edge.

High-Tech Features

- **Treated leathers:** Treated to improve water repellence and softness of kangaroo leather and cowhide.
- **Bladed outsoles:** With elongated and tapered studs for improved traction.
- **Synthetic uppers:** Once the mark of a cheap shoe, today's new synthetic microfiber uppers are lighter and more flexible. They hold shape and do not absorb much moisture, keeping the shoe light, but they don't breathe (vent moisture and heat) very well.
- **Sole and heel cushioning:** Various components, such as gels, cells, air, and foam, which add cushioning without raising the shoe too far off the ground and thus impairing performance.
- **Rubber jets and islands:** Introduced on the Adidas Predator in 1994, the claim is that the ribbed rubber patches sewn on the uppers will help players swerve the ball and increase the power of their shots.
- **Coatings:** A sticky polyurethane coating can be applied to synthetic shoe uppers to improve ball control. No claim for improved swerve, but tests show that the shoe grips the ball better in wet and dry conditions.
- **Banana lacing:** The laces and knot are shifted to the outside of the foot to create a broad, uninterrupted leather instep for improved touch; also called off-center or asymmetrical lacing.
- **Loop-lacing:** In loop-laced shoes, flat fabric loops replace traditional eyelets. As with banana lacing, the idea is to flatten and reduce excess material on the instep area.

Buying Shin Guards

Wearing shin guards is mandated by every youth soccer organization in the United States. Although wearing them doesn't guarantee that your child won't ever suffer a leg injury, they do reduce bruises and contusions to the shin and ankle. As with most protective equipment, don't skimp on price. The degree of protection is pretty much in direct proportion to the amount you pay. In addition, new technologies offer more protection than older designs. Expect to pay at least $15 or $20 for a good pair of shin guards.

Inexpensive shin guards are adequate for very young players because protection isn't as much of a concern as it is for older players, who can break a bone with a misplaced kick. Many of the low-end variety rely on wands, or plastic stiffeners, sewn into the shin guard. They don't offer the same protection as a guard with a hard shell, but may be fine for six- and seven-year-olds. Under no circumstances should a child of ten or older be permitted to wear a younger child's light-duty shin guards.

For younger players, shin guards that include ankle padding are a good choice. You don't want one or two kicks to the ankle to discourage your budding soccer enthusiast. It's also important for younger players to have guards that fit comfortably and are easy to put on. For the very young player, shin guards are part of the excitement of playing "real" soccer. If those guards are cumbersome or if they don't stay in place, that excitement will wear off quickly—and your child may not want to wear them.

As youngsters get older, they need shin guards that deliver higher performance. That translates to less weight and more comfort and protection. There are many technologies designed to deliver higher performance, including moldable layers of fiberglass (OSi), gel, and entrapped air cushioning systems. Beware of high-tech-sounding components, however, such as DuPont's Kevlar fiber (known for its use in bulletproof vests). The very small amount of Kevlar fiber used in shin guards does nothing to strengthen the product. The use of Kevlar has been a marketing ploy of shin-guard manufacturers for years.

High-performance guards designed with attached (or detachable) ankle guards offer Achilles tendon and forefoot padding, and often include cups or disks that protect the bones at either side of the ankle. Other high-performance shin guards, such as most OSi products that can be molded so they fit the contour of your child's shin, don't offer built-in ankle protection. Players who prefer these guards may decide to buy padded ankle guards that are sold separately or as part of a package.

For both younger and older players, it's important that shin guards stay in place. The old-fashioned way of securing shin guards—still preferred by some players—is athletic tape. But most shin guards come with straps and Velcro closures that do the job. Shin guards with attached ankle protectors stay in place better than others because they attach to the leg in two places—at the foot with a stirrup, and at the calf with a top strap. For guards without ankle protectors, compression sleeves are the best way to hold the shin guard to the leg. Compression sleeves are elastic tubes that can be purchased separately and used with any guard.

Shin Guard Shopper's Checklist

- **Size:** Guards come in various sizes. The hard portion of shin guards ranges from about 6.5 inches to 11 inches long. Buy a guard that covers the front of the leg to a height equal to the upper calf, according to the National Safe Kids Campaign. Coverage should extend to 2 to 3 inches above the foot.
- **Fit:** The shin guard should conform to the shape of your child's leg. When a shin guard is strapped in place, look for good contact with the leg.
- **Support:** Choose elastic straps (the wider the better) and Velcro closures that are comfortable, easy to use, and hold the guard securely in place.
- **Care:** You'll want shin guards that are easy to wash, either by hand or by machine. Look for a guard with a lining that's been treated with an antimicrobial agent to reduce odor.
- **Weight:** Don't buy a heavy shin guard—your child won't want to wear it. There are plenty of good choices under 6 ounces.
- **Hardness:** A hard shell offers the most protection. Press on the center of a shin guard with your thumbs, and you'll get an idea of how much protection it offers.
- **Water resistance:** Select shin guards that won't absorb a lot of water and become heavy on rainy days.
- **Comfort and safety:** To keep legs dry and cool, pick a shin guard that allows ventilation. Avoid guards with sharp edges that can cut your child or another player.
- **Low-profile:** Youth players want shin guards that don't interfere with running and are easy to pull socks over. (Guards should be worn under socks to help keep them in place and to prevent injuries due to a player's foot being snagged between the shin and shin guard.)

Buying Uniforms

Buying uniforms is different from purchasing other pieces of equipment because the style and maker are typically specified by the team or club. If you are asked for input, lobby for something that does not change from year to year and will stand up to repeated washings.

The most economical approach for recreation or in-house teams is to require the purchase of reversible jerseys. Our town uses the blue side for the "away" team and the white for the "home" side, as noted on our schedules. The shirts are durable enough so they can be worn by younger brothers, sisters, and neighbor children when they're outgrown.

Cotton T-shirts in various team colors are also a comfortable solution, but will typically require a new purchase every season or two.

Some travel and premier-level teams may buy their uniforms on their own. Typically, the team manager will ask for a volunteer to coordinate the effort. If you're the lucky one, get quotes from local retailers and check out the prices in soccer gear catalogs and on the Internet. Expect to pay about $40 to $70 per set (jersey, shorts, and socks) when ordering in quantity. Buying uniforms individually costs about 25 percent more. Having numbers and names screened on will add about $10. And don't forget that you'll need a home and an away jersey.

If ordering from a local soccer retailer, don't wait until August for the fall season or March for the spring season. Order early, and ask the retailer for a delivery date that is at least two weeks before you need the uniforms. This will allow time for parents to pick up the uniforms, make necessary exchanges and apply numbers, and so on.

Keeper Gloves

Gloves help keepers make saves because they grip the ball better than bare hands and increase the area with which to stop the ball. They also protect the hands from the sting of the ball. Most kids won't need them until their opponents can strike hard shots—at ten or eleven years old.

Tony DiCicco, who has been both goalkeeping coach and head coach of the U.S. Women's National Team, recommends that keeper gloves be purchased one size larger than needed. This is not to allow for growth. The extra half-inch fingertip length will help deflect shots that would otherwise end up in the net. The play (movement of the hand in the glove allowed by the extra size) also helps prevent the foam palms from tearing.

Using and Caring for Keeper Gloves

- Dampened gloves grip better than dry ones, so it's useful to keep a water bottle near the net to moisten the gloves as needed.
- Clean gloves last longer and grip better. Hand-wash gloves with a mild detergent and allow them to dry at room temperature.
- Gloves may be used even if the foam on the palm is partly worn off. Flaking, which sometimes occurs after just a few uses, does not impair performance.
- Keep two pairs of gloves—the best pair for match play, and the older pair for practice.

Choose gloves that are appropriate to your child's level of play. Expensive gloves have smooth palms made of thick, soft, spongy white latex foam. They provide more grip and shock absorption, but will wear out faster than more durable gloves with textured palms (that also cost less). For a recreation-level player, plan to spend $20 to $25 on a pair of gloves; for a travel player, $25 to $50. Pro-level models can cost well over $100.

Training Aids

Look at nearly any streetscape in the United States. Chances are you'll see a basketball hoop. Is it any wonder that the United States is the greatest basketball country in the world? Until the last five years, few backyards had the soccer equivalent to the basketball hoop—but that's changing. Today, dozens of companies sell rebounders, goals of various sizes, and other training devices.

Rebounders   The rebounder is essentially a portable kick wall. Made of netting fastened to a tubular metal frame, rebounders allow children to kick the ball at a target (the net) and have the ball bounce back to them. Better rebounders return the ball with enough speed so that the child has the added challenge of receiving the ball. The best rebounders have enough tension in the net so that the ball retains much of its original energy as it rebounds. Some models have high-tension netting, similar to the strings on a tennis racquet. With these units, a player can practice repetitive volleys or heading without ever letting the ball touch the ground.

Rebounders come in various sizes, ranging from 4 by 5 feet to 7 by 14 feet. With some models, the angle can be adjusted to change the way the ball returns—on the ground or in the air. Cost ranges from $150 to $500.

Portable Goals   Portable goals have the advantage of making practice more like a game. When a child scores, the ball hits the back netting in a satisfactory manner. But the ball does not return to the kicker, who must retrieve it, slowing down the action. Nevertheless, put one or two small goals in your backyard, and you can bet that your yard will be the most popular in the neighborhood.

The best size for young children (four to seven years) is 4 by 6 feet. Cost is about $200 per unit. For older kids or for larger backyard games, Kwik Goal, a manufacturer of goals and rebounders, recommends models that are 6.5 by 8.5 feet.

Tethered Balls Several manufacturers make a variation of this ball-on-a-cord product. The most popular brand, Soccer Pal, consists of a net for the ball and a short adjustable cord and handle. Kids are able to get dozens of touches on the ball in a minute. Advantages include low cost, usability in confined areas, and convenience in retrieving balls. Some of the skills that are well suited for practicing with a tethered ball include dribbling, moves, striking the ball with various parts of the foot, and volleys. There are many other drills you can do with a tethered ball. Soccer Pal includes a manual with the product.

CHAPTER 9

A Parent's Role

Soccer is a good sport for teaching your child about life. Between every pair of goals lie the joys of camaraderie, the demands of leadership, and the trials of character just waiting to be discovered. It's just as true, however, that soccer can foster wrongheadedness—blaming others for failure, undermining leadership, and grabbing attention with trash talk and red cards. Which lessons will your child learn? That depends largely on you.

To ensure a positive experience for your child, the first thing to remember is why kids want to play to begin with. Kids play soccer for enjoyment, pure and simple. The purpose of youth soccer isn't for parents to measure the athletic prowess of their children or for coaches to display their tactical brilliance. Nor is it to see which neighborhood, club, state, or region can produce the best teams.

Don't treat youth soccer as a means to an end. High school varsity teams, college athletic scholarships, and pro stardom are not the only reasons for encouraging your child to play soccer. If you need reasons to allow your child to play soccer beyond simple love of the game, remember that soccer rates high in player involvement, creativity, fitness, and fun.

More Competition May Not Be Better

The longer you are a soccer parent, the more you will hear the phrase "more competitive" used to describe the direction your child's soccer career ought to take. Many parents believe that a more competitive playing situation will develop children faster as players. They believe

that all the best kids (most athletic, most skilled) should play on the same team, and that all the best teams should play against the best teams. In this Darwinian view of soccer, the goal is to create a super team that can't be beaten. While such a policy may be good for a profit-driven professional club or for our national-team programs (another arena where a lot of money is at stake), it's not important for most youth players.

Studies show that given the choice between playing more or winning more, kids will choose playing. In one such study, the American Footwear Association surveyed more than 10,000 kids in grades 7 through 12 about why they played sports. Kids indicated that the number-one reason they play youth sports is to have fun. Motivations like playing with friends, staying fit, and improving skills are not far behind. In this survey, winning games was far down the list at number 10.

A Better Way

Instead of seeking a more competitive situation for a young player, look for a challenging situation. Challenge in sports comes from needing to solve problems in a fun, athletic environment.

Every program—even the very first season of recreation play—can be a challenging experience. Take, for example, a "noncompetitive" recreation team with one or two standout players, several average players, and a few weak or beginner players. The team may even be composed of kids who are not the same age. Put this team against a similarly composed team, and you produce a challenging situation for all the players. The top players must devise tactics to try to win. They must think for themselves. The middle-level players learn from the top players and are challenged to continue to improve. The team leaders must find ways to allow the weakest players to contribute. This situation most closely mimics the natural play "sandlot" environment that has served children well for generations and generations.

The key is to maintain a challenge. Today, many youth soccer organizations seek competition by putting all the best players on one team. The weaker players are put on weak teams or cut. Other organizations

Viewpoint: Youth Soccer Is Not a Ladder

Many people look at youth soccer as a ladder that a child must climb to be successful. At a young age, players begin with the least competitive level (recreation) and climb the rungs to the most competitive level (premier or ODP) as they get older. The less competitive programs and teams are thought of as preparation for more competitive programs and teams. For the kids who fall off the ladder—well, that's life. While this way of understanding youth soccer is fairly typical, it is not the only way to look at youth soccer.

I have withheld each of my children from playing at the premier level—and for us, it was the right decision. A surprising number of youth coaching directors and college coaches have done the same. Dr. Jay Martin, the varsity soccer coach at Ohio Wesleyan University and former president of the National Soccer Coaches Association of America, feels that premier puts too much emphasis on success at tournaments. He also believes that premier programs mislead parents when they promote themselves in ways that promise soccer scholarships from club-affiliated universities. Dean Conway, the coaching director for the Massachusetts Youth Soccer Association, declined to enroll his daughter in a premier program for similar reasons. Although he believes that a premier program, carefully administered, could be a positive experience, the reality is that most elite teams succumb to the parental mandate of winning games.

If your child insists on joining a premier team, delay permission to try out until age fourteen or fifteen. A recent study by the American Pediatrics Association says that concentration in one sport before age twelve, at a highly competitive level, can result in burnout and overuse injuries.

A child may choose to continue to play in a recreational program until well into the teen years. Club members who play on a B- or C-level travel team may prefer to continue at that level through high school, even though the A-team coach needs players to fill out the roster. Similarly, many youngsters opt not to play on a premier team because they find that their travel club experience is more rewarding, more fun, and the best way to improve as a player. Parents may prefer this, too, because there is less commitment of time and money.

seek to balance teams by distributing strong and weak players evenly. No one gets cut and everyone must play for at least half the game. In my experience, this latter approach is a more effective way to teach kids soccer. It's also the best way to nurture leadership, teamwork, and sportsmanship.

You'll have to decide whether to chase the holy grail of competitiveness—and which values you want your child to carry into adulthood.

Choosing a Coach

Find the right coach, and soccer can be a terrific experience for your child. Get stuck with the wrong coach, and it can be miserable. Take the time to make an informed decision about which coach will work with your child. Choice in many towns, where there are only one or two teams in an age group, is limited. Nevertheless, you should become knowledgeable about what to expect from a coach. It is better for a child to play recreational soccer with a coach who handles kids well but knows little about soccer than to play on a team coached by a maniac who dreams of being the next coach of DC United.

Before subjecting your child to a tryout, find out something about the individuals who coach in your child's age group. Ask how the tryouts will be run, whether there is a team manager, what the coach hopes to accomplish during the season, his number of years coaching, her playing time policy, and how many parents are "co-coaches"—and what their roles are. (More than one assistant coach is usually too many.) Ask questions of parents and kids who have played for the coach in the past.

Parents versus Paid Coaches For players under twelve years of age, the majority of teams are coached by volunteer parents. This system makes sense from an economic standpoint, puts less stress on kids, and furthers the soccer education of the parents who become involved. The downside is that many teams wind up with parents who don't know how to coach soccer, never played it, have no clue about how to work with large groups of children, and (in the worst cases) coach in order to ensure favored treatment of their child. The natural parental instinct, unfortunately, is often bent on creating a situation in which his child is the star.

Some leagues, tired of dealing with the minority of obnoxious, power-seeking parents, eliminate parent coaches altogether and rely on paid coaches instead. Paid coaches are typically young men and women who play for or coach at local universities and high schools. They typically know the game better than do most parents, but have had limited experience working with kids.

What's more, once a paycheck is involved, the potential for conflicting interests abound. Professional coaches often feel their mission, although not always stated clearly by the parents or club that has hired them, is to win games. Coaching to win games is often not the most effective way to develop players. In fact, it is often the reverse. Most experienced coaches know this, but not every paid coach is willing to stand up and say it, or to give up a few points in the win column for fear of being out of a job in the following season. Others don't care; to them, it's simply a paycheck.

In my experience, the ideal situation is to use parent coaches until age twelve. From twelve to fourteen or fifteen, a parent head coach with a professional (paid) trainer to help run the practices and to attend some matches is a good approach. The trainers are paid on an hourly basis and are assured of a minimum number of hours at the start of the season. The parent coach, of course, needs to have a strong knowledge of the game, be a good communicator, and be able to hold any lingering parental tendencies to favoritism in check. This maturity typically comes only after a parent has followed at least one child through the youth soccer system.

Once a child reaches high school age and demonstrates a desire to play at the most competitive level available, hiring a professional coach for training sessions and all matches may make sense.

The best sources for hiring experienced coaches are local colleges and universities. Your first choice would be the varsity head coach or assistant coach. If they are not available, ask if any of the players would be interested, and ask the head coach for a recommendation as to which player would be the best teacher. During my years as a parent coach, I was able to engage several pro trainers with excellent credentials, including a professional indoor player who eventually played for the MetroStars of Major League Soccer, the head varsity coach of a local university, and an All-American who had been a member of the Swedish youth national team.

Criteria for Hiring a Trainer or Coach If you have input in the decision about which coach to hire, here are five criteria by which to judge.

Soccer knowledge   Soccer knowledge is essential. Ideally, you want someone who has thought about how to teach tactics and skills—not only someone who has played the game. The trainer or coach should have participated in a licensing program. These programs should spell out what is appropriate to teach at various ages. There are several types of coach licenses, including state licenses for beginner (E and F) and intermediate (D) coaches; national licenses for more experienced coaches (A, B, C); and national youth coaching licenses. The national youth licensing program is relatively new and is geared specifically to coaches who train youth players.

Playfulness   The point of sports is to have fun. Some coaches have a special talent for making even the most tiresome drill fun. Look for a coach who is fit and who likes to join in with the kids and kick the ball around with them. The ones who stand on the sidelines, however knowledgeable, are simply not as much fun for kids.

Ability to teach   The best teachers get excited about seeing a child learn a new skill or draw an insight. Only boring teachers seem to enjoy hearing themselves lecture. Find a coach who gets excited about the knowledge the team is sharing, and you've found a coach your child is likely to learn from.

Perspective   The coach who lusts after winning records and state championships is one to avoid. Instead, seek out coaches who understand that winning in soccer is a matter of seeing young people enjoy the sport into their teen years and beyond.

Interest in children   Look for someone who is more interested in talking to your child than in talking to you. If after five or ten minutes with a group of kids, the candidate knows the players' first names, it's likely that you've found your coach.

How to Be a Team Manager

Typically, most of the work of running a soccer team has fallen on the shoulders of the coach and the coach's spouse or the coach and an assistant coach. They are in charge of making and distributing schedules, field assignments for practices and matches, directions to away games and tournaments. They also do paperwork associated with registering players, organize phone trees and fund-raising efforts, pay refs, buy equipment, attend club meetings, disseminate information about clinics, sign up for tournaments, get permission to travel out of state, and make the necessary travel arrangements. Plus a lot more: keeping the first-aid kit stocked, making sure corner flags are on hand for matches, checking to see if goals are secured to the ground, having water on hand at all times, assigning parents to bring oranges and juice for halftime, and organizing postseason parties.

As clubs and teams evolve and the time any single family can devote to volunteering shrinks, the informal arrangement of leaving the details to one or two families is giving way to the idea of a team manager or team parent. Team managers are responsible for all of the tasks mentioned in this section, but don't do it all themselves. Instead, they delegate the various tasks to parents on the team.

Tips for Team Managers At the beginning of the season, the team manager should call a team meeting and ask for volunteers to handle the various assignments. This approach works great if the parents are a cohesive bunch who socialize with one another through the community or schools. If you don't have a group with that sort of chemistry, it is harder to get volunteers, so you may simply have to assign jobs—or else the work will end up falling back on the shoulders of two or three people, almost certainly including you and your spouse—so the incentive to make this work is strong.

To manage a team, divide all of the various tasks into jobs. Assign one job to each family at your first team meeting, and supply them with printed job descriptions. Jobs should include the following:

- **Manager**—Handles all schedules and directions and everything that someone else doesn't handle.
- **Bookkeeper**—Collects money and writes checks.
- **Communications coordinator**—Makes calls, sends e-mail and faxes.
- **Drinks and snacks coordinator**—Assigns drinks and snacks to team families and may also be put in charge of social events.
- **Team nurse**—Maintains and brings the first-aid kit to games and practices and ensures there is enough water and ice.
- **Tournament coordinator**—Identifies possible tournaments, polls parents as to interest, and makes travel arrangements.
- **Team registrar**—Works with the club registrar to take care of registration and getting passes.

You may also want to put families in charge of equipment and safety, publicity, and fund-raising. For big jobs, assign two or three families.

Viewpoint: An Effective but Controversial Solution

Have you ever seen the *Family Circus* cartoon panel that shows the children watching professionals play soccer on television? The caption reads, "The reason they can play so good is that their parents aren't yelling at them from the sidelines."

It's funny, sad, and all too true. Parents and coaches often cloud the sunny experience of youth soccer. They don't mean to, but they do. For years, youth soccer organizations have sought ways to make parents and coaches understand that the goal of their programs is for kids to learn the game while having fun. Sometimes it takes years for the message to get through, and by that time, it's often too late. The thousands of new coaches and parents that must be educated each year compound the problem.

But there is some good news.

Carl Pavlovich and Al Soper of the Northern Ohio Girls Soccer League (NOGSL) came up with an idea that works—and works quickly! At games played on what they called Silent Sunday, parents and coaches were not allowed to yell, cheer, or shriek when goals were scored. They were not allowed to give instructions. They could only applaud.

The aim of the program was to allow players to make their own decisions, improve communication on the field, and eliminate verbal questioning of the refs' calls. NOGSL board members felt that parents and coaches were inadvertently hurting player development by their sideline intervention. They were also worried about the high dropout rate of youth referees caused by the verbal assaults of spectators and coaches.

Silent Sunday was approved in July 1999, and a mailing went out to coaches and clubs explaining the program and its goals. Referees would be permitted to ask any offending coach or parent to leave the field if interference persisted after one warning.

Web Sites Make Life Easier With the popularity of the Internet, team management is changing once again. There are several Web sites that can help a team manage itself, not to mention provide e-mail. Several youth sports dot-coms will allow you to create a team Web site. Such sites give team members and their parents a way to communicate quickly and efficiently. They can include rosters with phone numbers and addresses, team and tournament schedules, directions to matches, game-day weather forecasts, match results and league standings,

Not all coaches and parents liked the program. Some thought players wouldn't know what to do without "help" from the sidelines. Others claimed they had a "right" to cheer. Nevertheless, the program went forward.

Silent Sunday took place October 3, 1999, in NOGSL's sixty-five communities. Happily, there were no incidents. A few warnings were issued by refs, but not one coach or parent had to be asked to leave a field. Some parents even got into the spirit of the program by sticking lollipops in their mouths or wearing surgical masks. Others held up signs with messages such as GREAT SHOT and NICE TOUCH to let their cheers be "heard."

Soper said that when he walked up to the first field he visited that day, he was struck by the fact that he could hear players talking—something he couldn't recall hearing before.

The quiet was eerie for refs, too. One found it hard to get into the game because there was no reaction from the sidelines when he blew his whistle. But it didn't take long for him to enjoy reffing without the heckling.

Many coaches commented that the experience was positive. One six-year coaching veteran said Silent Sunday made her rethink her coaching style. Others enjoyed being able to sit back, watch the game, and take notes for what to work on during the following week's practice.

Players loved the program. They thought it was fun to play without distracting sideline instruction and comments. Some asked if every game day could be silent.

The effects of Silent Sunday spilled over to the games that were played in the weeks that followed. Parents were quieter, and there was less coaching from the sidelines. In addition, the number of youth refs who signed up actually increased the following season.

NOGSL has staged additional Silent Sundays. Many other leagues around the country have since joined in.

individual stats, and even action photos from the last match. These Web sites will give you the tools to create your own site and advice about what to include. The best-known of these sites is *eteamz.com*.

Problems with Parents

Incidents of poor behavior on the part of parents and coaches at youth sporting events have increased in the last ten years. Whether you blame

Eight Ways to Ensure a Good Experience

1. *Choose the right playing situation:* **While your child is young, your job as a soccer parent is to help your child choose the appropriate level of play and a suitable team. Remember, a child starting on a B-level team improves faster—and has more fun—than a child who rides the bench on an A-level team.**

2. *Play soccer with your child:* **Nothing will add more to your child's enjoyment of the sport than having you as a playmate. Learn the skills and moves together. Help perfect techniques by adding a kick wall or a rebounder to your backyard. Take your child to local parks and look for pickup games with other children.**

3. *Ensure safety:* **Don't leave safety up to the coach and referee only—it's everyone's responsibility. When you arrive for a match, be on the lookout for unsafe situations such as unanchored goals, a drainage grate near the sideline, or broken glass or stones on the field. Instruct your child to avoid horseplay before, during, and after the match.**

4. *Set a sportsmanlike example:* **Be a good host when welcoming visiting teams' parents at home matches. Say hello; ask how their kids' season is going. Offer to buy a round of coffee. And when the game heats up, remember that just because the parents are from another town, that doesn't make them your mortal enemies.**

5. *Help run the team:* **If your child plays on a travel team, help out. Learn what's involved in club administration and find a way to help. The more assistance teams and clubs get from parents, the more they can do to help youth players.**

them on the stress of living two-income lifestyles or the pressure to see kids succeed or the banalities of Jerry Springer and the WWF, it's true in every youth sport, not just soccer.

The higher the competitive level, the more chance for problems. In recreation soccer, with the youngest kids, adult behavior rarely gets out of hand. In leagues for older children, it can become very unpleasant. Sometimes referees will ask offending parents or coaches to leave the game.

Parents instinctively want the best for their children. If they feel their child is being treated unfairly or threatened, they react angrily and irrationally. Typically the problems are limited to verbal assaults by coaches, parents, and players on referees and on the opposing

Sought-after skills include bookkeeping, fund-raising, scheduling, team Web site maintenance, and making travel arrangements. If you can't take on a big job right now, do a small one, such as assigning responsibility for halftime refreshments or hosting a postseason party.

6. *Encourage your child to help younger players:* This is a great way to bring out the best in your child. Once children have a few years of playing experience, they make great volunteers because they're really beginning to understand the sport. Youth referees, assistant referees, and assistant coaches are in great demand. Looking for something less formal? Suggest that your child organize a backyard 3v3 tournament for neighborhood tykes.

7. *Be supportive of your child's team:* Recognize the achievements of the team and of the individuals on the team, not only those of your child. Avoid negative commentary about refs, coaches, and players. And the next time you're standing on the sidelines, relax and enjoy the game. Don't embarrass your child by becoming a loudmouth parent.

8. *Set a healthy example:* If mom or dad serve it, it's got to be good. That's what kids believe—even if it's not what their health teacher says! So keep fatty and sweet foods to a minimum, and be sure your kids get the bulk of their calories from carbohydrates such as vegetables and grains. Restrict your alcohol consumption and shun cigarettes, especially in front of kids at matches and team gatherings.

coaches, parents, and players. Sometimes shouting matches lead to grudges, broken friendships, or—worse—to violence.

Watch Soccer on TV

Watching a soccer game on TV is a great way for a child to learn about the game. A young fan can learn skills and tactics, and even be inspired by seeing a fancy move.

Professional soccer games on TV are more readily available than ever before. Check listings on U.S. Soccer's Web site *(www.ussoccer.com)* for national team matches or the Major League Soccer site *(www.mlsnet.com)* for MLS games. In addition to local cable coverage, many games can be seen on ABC, ESPN, ESPN Classic, ESPN2, and Tele-mundo, the Spanish-language network.

Take Your Child to the Stadium

What's even better than watching a game on TV with your child? Attending a game in person. You have lots of matches to choose from, including local high school, college, amateur, and pro-league matches. Watch for national-team and professional matches in your area, too.

Going to a game allows you and your child to get to see more of what players "off the ball" (that is, away from the action) are doing.

Plus, you can't beat the sights and sounds of actually being at a sporting event. And no sporting events are more fun than soccer games. If you've ever been to a World Cup game or watched one on TV, you know how exciting the atmosphere is. Whistles are blowing. Drums are beating. Flags and signs are waving. Fans are singing and chanting. It's quite a show!

Big games can draw very large crowds. More than 200,000 people were at the Brazil–Uruguay 1950 World Cup final in Brazil. A full-capacity crowd of 75,000 watched France and Brazil play in the 1998 World Cup final. And 90,185 fans were on hand for the 1999 Women's World Cup final at the Rose Bowl—the largest crowd ever for a women's sporting event. Even President Clinton was there.

Eating and Drinking for Success

Your child can't play to full potential without eating and drinking properly. The night before a game or practice is the time to stock up on complex carbohydrates, because these are what give your child energy. Foods like pasta, bread, and rice will provide plenty of fuel. Fruits and vegetables are also a good source of complex carbohydrates. Avoid simple carbohydrates, which are high in sugar and don't provide the long-term energy your child will need. Protein from meat and other foods is also good, but in limited amounts. Avoid fats and sweets if possible. A good example of a healthy meal is pasta with grilled chicken, bread, a salad, fruit, and a glass of skim milk.

The morning before the game you should still be focused on complex carbohydrates. Avoid fatty foods like sausage and home fries because they take longer to digest and can cause cramping. Pancakes with a little syrup (and no butter!), unsweetened cereal with skim milk, or a bagel with jelly are good choices. Try to have breakfast at least one to two hours before the game.

The closer it gets to playing time, the smaller your child's portion should be. For snacks, stay away from junk food and instead try celery sticks, pretzels, low-fat popcorn, oranges, or other high-carbohydrate, low-fat foods. Less than one hour before playing, your child shouldn't have any food and should focus on getting properly hydrated.

Teach your child to drink plenty of fluids before the game and as often as possible during the game. Remind children that they should drink even if they don't feel thirsty. Cool (not cold) water or sports drinks are the best choices for fluids during the game.

After the game is when players should fill up on meat and other protein-rich foods, which will help build and repair muscles. This is the time when they can indulge in that cheeseburger or pizza they've been craving. If they have to play again the next day, though, keep focusing on complex carbohydrates.

CHAPTER 10

Being the Coach

Coaching my kids' teams has been a rewarding experience. I was able to spend a lot of time with each child, meet other families in the area, and improve my soccer knowledge at the same time. Coaching also enabled me to be a part of the lives of many other children—and to then watch them mature into adults. Hardly a week goes by when I don't bump into one of the many children I have coached over the years, many of whom are now in high school, college, or the workforce.

When I began coaching, I was not very good at it. My idea of coaching was based on my first experiences of being coached, when I was a ten-year-old child. The trouble was, I was coaching first-graders. As noted in chapter 3, there are stages in the development of children that should be considered by those who try to teach them. Like thousands of others I had no clear knowledge of this, and treated the six-year-olds like ten-year-olds. To complicate matters, in any group there will be two or three six-year-olds with the maturity of older kids and two or three with that of younger kids.

I remember one little seven-year-old named Greg. He had no idea of teamwork, but he liked to score goals. At practice, he paid little attention to the dribbling races I had planned or my discourses on the importance of passing. When I turned my head, he went back to shooting goals. During our matches, Greg would stay near the goal and pounce on the ball when it came near—even if it meant taking it from a teammate. He would then dribble to the goal and shoot.

During our two seasons together, Greg was our team's leading scorer. After every game, I'd say, "Nice goals, Greg, but you'd be more valuable to the team if you learned to pass." When the third season came around, I was surprised to learn that Greg had decided not to play soccer anymore. My guess is that if I knew then what I know now, Greg might still be playing—and scoring goals.

Who Should Coach?

Over the years, I've met a lot of parent coaches; some were terrific coaches and others less so. The best coaches have the desire to do two things: to nurture kids and to share their soccer knowledge. Poor coaches deliver too much of one (either one) and not enough of the other.

If you feel you can deliver both, volunteer. Youth soccer needs you. If your knowledge is good but your skills with kids are weak, enroll in a course that will help you understand the needs of children at the ages with which you hope to work. If you're weak in your soccer knowledge, attend clinics and licensing programs, look for adult pickup games to play in, and watch matches live and on TV. Then apply as an assistant to a knowledgeable veteran coach from whom you can learn.

Should You Coach If You've Never Played? Only as a last resort should parents who have never played soccer try to become coaches. There are lots of other ways to get involved. For example, you can be an assistant or a team manager. It's a hard thing for enthusiastic parents to understand that they are not qualified to coach their child's soccer team because they never played—especially if they have experience playing and coaching other sports. But in my experience you're better off if you can find volunteers who have played to do the job. Kids want to learn the game. They want an adult who can teach skills and tactics. Don't allow your enthusiasm to be a coach blind you to these simple facts. If you are forced to coach because no one else is available, make it your first order of business to find a couple of high school players who would like to volunteer to help out.

The Next Generation of Parents Soccer has suffered from the fact that many parents never played the sport. That's changing—a new generation of parents who played soccer through their youth in the '70s and '80s are having children—and those kids are getting to the age when they can sign up to play in a youth league. These parents—perhaps you are among them—will change the face of youth soccer. No longer will children be coached by well-intentioned novice coaches who are trying to adapt what they know of coaching traditional sports, such as football or baseball, to soccer.

Choosing an Assistant Coach It's helpful, though not necessary, to have an assistant coach. If you decide you need one, choose someone who shares your philosophy about coaching and with whom you feel you communicate well. Your choice should complement your abilities. For example, if you're a male coaching females, choose a female assistant. If you have a long commute to work or must be away on business travel from time to time, choose someone who works close to home. If you have excellent soccer knowledge but not much experience with kids, choose someone who has worked with kids.

Avoid selecting an assistant who feels it's necessary to call instructions to players during matches. And avoid having more than one assistant.

Planning Your Practices

Think of yourself as more of a facilitator than a coach. Your job is to teach in a way that allows kids to learn and have fun at the same time—not to plan strategies to win games.

In fourteen years of coaching girls and boys of every age from six to seventeen, I've probably run nearly a thousand training sessions. The format I use—and the one recommended by many youth soccer educators—is fairly simple:

Get kids engaged in a fun, simple game. (5 minutes) Get kids involved as soon as they arrive to practice. Plan games that allow players to warm up and make the mental transition to soccer. For kids who have learned the basic passing and receiving skills, I usually have players form groups and play 2v5 in a circle. (Groups of 4v2 or 3v1 also work.) Have five kids make a small circle about 7 or 8 yards in diameter. Put two kids in the center. The players on the outside of the circle pass to each other in any order. The ones in the circle try to intercept or deflect the passes. If a player in the center wins or deflects the ball, the player who has been in the center the longest joins the ring of players and

Figure 10.1:
The "Circle" game is a great warm-up for a practice.

sends the player who made the poor pass to the center. First pass is free (not contended). Once kids know the game, they can form groups on their own.

Do stretching exercises. (5–10 minutes) Young kids don't really need to stretch before play, but stretching is a good habit to get into for when they're older. I usually put one child in charge and use the opportunity to explain the focus of the day's session and to make team announcements. Include stretches for all of the muscle groups, from the neck to the toes, but tell kids not to bounce or pull so hard they feel discomfort. Allow older kids to stretch for longer periods.

Demonstrate one individual skill (or two related skills), a combination play, or a simple tactic. (5–10 minutes) Most coaching manuals recommend focusing on one subject per session. Because soccer skills are closely interrelated, however, you will be able to focus on one skill and review one that was learned at an earlier session at the same time. For example, while teaching chipping, you may want to review chest receptions. While working on corner kicks, you may also be able to practice volleys.

Many demonstrations involve more than one person, so it helps to have a knowledgeable assistant coach. You can, of course, select players to help with the demonstration as well. For very young players, the demonstration may be showing how to make a push pass or inside-of-foot reception. For older kids, it may be making wall passes or crossing from the flanks while dribbling under pressure.

Have kids practice what has been demonstrated. (5–10 minutes) This part of the practice often requires areas or spots to be marked with cones. If possible, lay out your cones before practice so you don't have to stop and waste time. If this isn't possible, enlist the aid of your assistant coach or players to set up the cones.

Have kids play a game designed to incorporate what has been demonstrated. (10 minutes) There is a real art to devising and selecting the appropriate game for purposes of practicing skills and learning tactics. Build a library of games that work for you. You can see them demonstrated at clinics (often staged in connection with annual state meetings and at national coaches' conventions). You can also find them in books, magazines, videos, CDs, and now on the Internet. (See appendix C.)

Have kids play a small-sided game. (10–20 minutes) This game can be a regular soccer scrimmage (for example, two games of 4v4), or it can be a soccerlike game (see the "Three-Team Soccer" section at the end of chapter 4)—as long as it includes finishing. Many of today's national coaches lament that the U.S. youth soccer system produces lots of midfielders, defenders, and keepers—but not many strikers. They recommend that you incorporate finishing in this and other portions of your training sessions.

Cool down and make announcements to players and parents. (5–10 minutes) Use this time to review with players what they've learned during the session. Remind them about upcoming practices, matches, or other team events. Older players should use this time to stretch muscles to prevent stiffness later.

Advice for Successful Practices

My most successful practices tend to be the ones I plan ahead of time. My poorest are those that I plan in my head while rushing from my job to the field. For young kids, the sessions center around a basic skill (such as finishing) or a combination of skills (such as passing and receiving). For older kids, the focus is on a simple tactic, such as executing a wall pass or free kick, maintaining possession on throw-ins, or defending corner kicks. I try to concentrate on only one—or at most, two skills or tactical problems—per session; trying to do too much in one practice causes the players to become distracted and to lose interest.

Following the demonstration segment of the practice, it's often helpful to break the team into small groups. This is when an assistant comes in handy. But an assistant can't be of much help without knowing what you've planned. Try to talk about your plan before practice, ideally the day before, so the assistant can give you some input or ask questions. Worst case, you both need to arrive at practice ten minutes early to go over the practice plan.

During practices, coaches should try to keep kids moving. Brief rests of thirty to sixty seconds are sufficient, with perhaps one longer break of three to five minutes. Try to simulate the rhythm and pace of a match in your training sessions. The average length of a session for young kids should be about fifty minutes. For older kids, the practices range from sixty to seventy-five minutes. Generally, your practices should not last longer than your matches.

You can recognize an inexperienced or ignorant coach if you see lines of kids, five or six deep, awaiting their turn to perform a drill or exercise or listening to endlessly detailed instructions. Besides keeping all the kids moving, you should keep your verbal instructions to a minimum. We've all seen how fidgety kids get with coaches who insist on giving long-winded explanations. I try not to exceed three or four minutes of talk before getting to the action.

There are several effective ways, however, to make your points. When kids are practicing what has been demonstrated, stay free to roam from pair to pair or group to group and offer individual critiques. Tell the kids to freeze if you blow your whistle during soccerlike games

such as keep-away. While they're frozen, quickly deliver your observation or ask for a child's opinion of the positions, and then resume play.

The most effective way by far for communicating ideas to kids, however, is to join in the game. It's amazing how much you can tell—and show—kids while you're running around with them. It's also amazing how well they listen when you become one of them.

Teaching Heading

Heading, as mentioned earlier, is a concern for youth soccer parents, coaches, and administrators. Most doctors say there is no cause for alarm—but there are several things that parents and coaches can do to minimize the risks associated with the technique.

For kids under nine, teach proper technique with lightweight balls such as Nerf soccer balls, size 3 balls, or even balloons. This allows the child to perfect technique without anxiety about getting hit in the face with the ball.

Introduce heading with age-appropriate balls when kids need this skill to play—not usually before ten years old. Before that, there are few chances to head the ball because, aside from punts, few balls are driven into the air.

In your training sessions, focus on proper technique. Tell players that they can minimize impact to the head by using their bodies to help absorb the ball's impact.

Minimize the number of repetitions with real balls during training. Instead, work on timing using lightweight balls.

Teach players how to become skillful at receiving the ball with their chests and feet. Good receiving skills will give the players confidence to attempt to control the ball instead of aimlessly pounding it upfield with their heads.

Stress the benefits of keeping the ball on the ground. Balls on the ground are easier to handle by teammates, and are unlikely to promote collisions between the head and other hard objects.

Instruct kids to avoid unnecessary headers. It is a wasted opportunity to head the ball into the midst of a team's defense. It's usually better to gain control of the ball and then pass it to a teammate.

Identify dangerous heading situations that can result in concussions. For example, players will often "help" a weak clearance or service into the goal area by flicking it backward with their head. Typically, they do not know if there is an opponent behind them also trying to reach the ball. By recognizing the dangers of such situations, players may take precautions, such as glancing back before heading the ball. The player "behind" the header learns to keep a safe distance.

On rare occasions, concussions may be caused when a player is unexpectedly struck in the head by the ball. Teach players that when defenders are under pressure, they often resort to trying to blast the ball clear. If players are alert and ready, they may be able to avoid being hit in the head from close range.

Head Protection Doesn't Help, and May Actually Hurt Several products, ranging from helmets to padded headbands, have been marketed with claims of lessening the impact of headers and head collisions. For players under nine, they are not needed because the ball is rarely in the air. For older kids, headgear would drastically change the nature of the game, except perhaps for goalkeepers. And experts debate whether such a step is necessary even for them.

So far, many neurologists are skeptical about the value of such products. They point out that it is the movement of the brain inside the skull that causes concussions and damage. Protecting the outer surface of the head does little to cushion what's happening inside the skull. Some doctors speculate that adding weight to the head, even in the form of protection, may increase head mass and cause neck injuries. Furthermore, protective headgear may embolden kids to be more aggressive when heading the ball, leading to additional injuries.

The Coach's Role at Matches

The best youth coaches decide on positions, game tactics, and substitutions ahead of time. This enables them to sit on the bench with their subs and assistant, calmly focusing on the match. There is little that can be communicated or taught from the sidelines during play—practice is the time for that. Coaches who feel they can gain an edge for their players by cheering and yelling instructions, cajoling or arguing with referees, and trading barbed remarks with opposing coaches are missing the point. It's the kids' game once the whistle blows to start the match. So relax and keep a pad and pencil handy to jot down notes during the course of the match. Kids like to hear specific comments about their play—especially when they do something right.

The USYSA requests coaches to teach players to behave with reasonable restraint (and to conduct themselves likewise) at matches. The principles are as follows:

- Play according to the rules in a sportsmanlike manner.
- Do not question calls by the ref or encourage players, parents, and spectators to do so. Ask for clarification of rulings during an official break or when indicated by the ref only.
- Ensure that any coaching you do from the sideline is informative and instructive. Haranguing is not permitted. Coaching must be done from the bench area and the correct sideline. Do not surround the field with assistant coaches whose role it is to bark instructions as the kids draw near.

- Coaches are responsible for the conduct of players, parents, and spectators. A ref who feels that the coach has not adequately controlled parents or spectators may issue a caution or ejection to the coach as well as to the offender.

Fostering Leadership and Teamwork

Sports can be a great stage for teaching leadership and teamwork skills to children, but it's helpful for a coach to understand team dynamics to facilitate learning. A team is made up of individuals. Teamwork occurs when those individuals work together to accomplish a common goal.

Fostering leadership and building teamwork is tricky business for a coach. There are three common approaches: Do nothing and allow the kids to find their respective roles on the team themselves—just as they would if left on their own in the backyard without adult supervision.

Second, build unity by stressing group pride, often at the expense of the individual stars. Team discipline, paying dues, snappy uniforms and matching warm-up suits, eating together at tournaments, team cheers . . . you get the picture.

I've tried a third (and more middle-of-the-road) course, deferring to the natural child leader when feasible. Leaders are usually the best all-around players and the players all the others respect and listen to. There can, however, be several leaders on a team, including offensive and defensive leaders, as well as on-field and off-field leaders. Whether there's one leader or several, respect the fledgling efforts of young leaders and give them room to exercise their abilities.

Aside from leaders, there are other important team roles. They include morale boosters, players who lift spirits and maintain perspective—often with a sense of humor; scorekeepers and timekeepers who quantify players' abilities and keep track of the team's progress; and managers-in-training who keep things running smoothly, suggest water breaks, watch for book bags that others might forget or trip over. Sometimes the team leader or another player adopts the role of teacher or communicator. These are the kids who explain what the coaches or leaders want and are adept at painting word pictures. Perhaps the most prized player on a team, aside from the leader, is the idea giver. These players generate ideas and solutions to problems—and offer them to the leader and group to decide which are the best ones to try. Finally, there are the mediators, players who can settle disputes quickly and fairly.

Allow players to assume roles for which they are suited, and your coaching experience will be a joy.

Soccer Safety

Whether you're a coach or a parent, you should think in terms of safety before, during, and after practices and games. Tape a copy of the boxed safety checklist (at right) to a clipboard and consult it every time you take the field.

Where and When Most Serious Accidents Occur In my years of coaching I've seen broken legs, concussions due to head-to-head collisions, and plenty of cuts, sprains, strains, blisters, and bruises. Little could have been done to prevent them. But I've also seen high winds blow over a goal—just missing a player. The most serious accidents in soccer occur with goals, and these are preventable.

Goals must be securely anchored to the ground, either with weighted bags or stakes. Don't play or practice with unanchored goals.

Surprisingly, however, goals are at their most dangerous when games are not being played and practice is not in session, according to Andy Caruso, former chairman of the Soccer Industry Council of America's committee on safety. Accidents occur when goals fall on kids while being moved before or after games and practices, especially when being moved without adult supervision.

Most of the goal-related injuries and deaths have involved home-made goals. They are heavier and thus more difficult to handle safely than commercially manufactured portable goals.

According to Caruso, padding of goalposts is of dubious value. It may make keepers more fearless about diving near the post. He also speculates that padded posts, due to dampened rebounds, will increase the number of loose balls in the goal area, causing more collisions between keepers, defenders, and strikers.

Most Common Injuries and How to Handle Them Injuries are an unfortunate part of youth soccer. Sprains and strains, especially to the legs and feet, are two of the most common injuries.

A *sprain* is a stretched or torn ligament. (Ligaments are the bands of connective tissue that join bones together. They help stabilize the joints.) Signs of a sprain are pain, bruising, and swelling. The player will usually feel a tear or pop in the joint. Severe sprains produce intense pain, as the ligament tears completely or separates from the bone. When this happens, the joint becomes nonfunctional. In moderate sprains there is some tearing of the ligament and instability in the joint. In mild sprains the ligaments are stretched but not torn, and the joint remains stable.

Safety Checklist

- Goals are anchored with anchor pegs or weighted bags to prevent tipping or blowing over. Unanchored goals can easily topple in high winds, while children climb upon them, or if children attempt to move them without adult supervision.

- Goals are made to today's standards. Homemade goals, often fabricated in local workshops, may have protruding bolts, net hooks, or anchor stakes that can cause severe injuries.

- Players are not wearing jewelry such as necklaces, wristwatches, bracelets, or earrings. Jewelry can become ensnared during play, causing injury.

- Warm-up area is clear of soccer bags and other items that could cause someone to trip. Many injuries happen before the match even begins. Keep warm-up areas clear.

- Benches, bleachers, and spectators are not too close to the sideline. The first 5 yards from the sideline should be kept clear to prevent mishaps and to allow players enough room to throw the ball back into play.

- There are water bottles for everyone—or a large jug and cups. It should be a parent's or coach's responsibility to have water at every match.

- Players are wearing sunscreen to prevent sunburn. Use team dues to purchase several containers of sunscreen and store them in the team's first-aid kit.

- First-aid kit is complete, and there is plenty of ice on hand. Your first-aid kit should include bandages, tape, gauze pads, cold packs, non-aspirin pain reliever, scissors, sting reliever, sunscreen, elastic wrap, and closure clips. Ice is invaluable for treating bumps and sprains, reducing swelling.

- No poison ivy, poison oak, poison sumac, stinging nettles, or other dangerous plants are around the field perimeter. Warn kids about what they may encounter while retrieving balls.

- Field is free of potentially harmful objects. These include damaged or inflexible corner flags that will not bend if fallen upon, stones, broken glass and other debris on or near the playing field, drainage grates, or exposed irrigation sprinkler heads.

- Players are wearing adequate shin guards under long socks. Socks help keep shin guards in place, preventing trips.

Viewpoint: On Being the Assistant Coach

During my years of youth coaching, I have sometimes found myself in the unenviable position of being the assistant coach. It has never been a very fun job—the head coach is the one who gets to do the cool stuff, like coming up with lineups and deciding when to make substitutions. The assistant coach has to look official while doing dumb things like knowing how many seconds are left until halftime and chasing balls during shooting practice.

The first time I was an assistant coach, I figured it was my job to holler instructions to players at matches when the head coach's voice gave out. By my next assistant job, I had learned it was better to keep my mouth shut and to just work at keeping the first-aid kit stocked and the area around the bench free of orange peels and paper cups.

When my daughter's coach asked me to be the new assistant coach last season, I told him it wasn't something that I was dying to do. He asked me to think about it, and I eventually broke down and agreed—and it worked out much better than my earlier attempts at the job. What I came up with will, I trust, help hapless assistant coaches everywhere: stop thinking of yourself as just one more team cheerleader and start thinking of yourself as a game analyst.

At every game, I arrived armed with pad and pen. I would park myself on one end of the bench and concentrate on watching the match and taking notes. When

A *strain* is a pulled or torn muscle or tendon. (Tendons are the cords of tissue that connect muscles to bone.) Typical symptoms include pain, muscle spasm, muscle weakness, swelling, and cramping. In severe strains, the muscle or tendon is partially or completely torn, often incapacitating the player. In moderate strains, the muscle or tendon is overstretched and slightly torn, and some muscle function is lost. With a mild strain, the muscle or tendon is stretched slightly.

For all but the mildest sprain or strain, your child should see a doctor. Until you can get to the doctor, follow the "RICE" method:

- **Rest:** Immobilize the injured area and have your child sit quietly.
- **Ice:** Apply an ice pack (wrapped in a towel) to the injured area for ten to fifteen minutes.
- **Compression:** Wrap the injured area with elastic bandages.
- **Elevation:** Raise the injured area above the heart.

I saw a player do something well—or poorly—I'd jot it down. If a series of good passes created a goal-scoring opportunity, I'd scribble down a description of how it happened. If our defense broke down, I'd try to figure out why. In addition, I'd keep track of things like corner kicks, near-post shots versus far-post shots, and good clearances versus bad clearances.

At halftime, after the head coach had spoken his piece, I'd tell the players what I'd seen. Often, I'd mention names, always mixing you-shoulda's with praise for what they did well. I'd try to say something about the play of every player. After the first game or two, I noticed that the kids were actually listening to what I had to say—probably the first time in my coaching career that I had the undivided attention of players during my halftime or postgame talks. Subs, sitting with me on the bench during the match, began to crane their necks to check out what I was writing. Players started to ask me questions about specific plays and what else they might have tried in various situations.

Not only did I actually feel useful, but I also began to feel much more relaxed at games. Instead of becoming emotionally involved, as I often did in the past as head coach, I could stay objective and clearly see what was happening on the field. I felt no anguish when the other team scored and no wild jubilation when our girls did. In short, I felt more like a teacher—a good goal for a youth coach.

Over the next two or three days, continue to apply ice to the injured area several times a day, but only for ten to fifteen minutes at a time. Once the swelling and tenderness have subsided, you may want to try soaks in warm water or local heat application to reduce tightness or stiffness. Never apply heat while swelling is still present.

Camps, Tournaments, and Tours

I f playing during the regular soccer seasons does not give your child enough soccer, soccer camps, tournaments, and soccer tours offer other opportunities to play and learn. Camps and tours are primarily held in the summer, although some are also offered during spring school vacations. Tournaments are held year-round, but mostly in the spring and fall.

Soccer Camps

Say "camp" to a youth soccer player, and you're not likely to hear about pitching tents, lighting fires, toasting marshmallows, telling ghost stories, or swatting bugs. Expect stories about kicking balls, learning skills, and meeting new friends. . . .

Not so long ago, soccer camp was simply a place to stay for a week and play soccer. Today, there are not only more soccer camps, but more types of soccer camps than teams in the World Cup! Which one is right for your child?

Day Camps Day camps are ideal for young, beginning players. For many kids, day camps are their first camp experience. These camps focus on learning basic skills and having fun. Day camps are a good choice for little kids who want to go to camp but aren't ready to leave home and for older ones who might not have the time or money to go away.

Day camps run all day or half a day, usually at a nearby school or park. They are easy to get to and aren't as expensive as overnight camps. Day camps may be sponsored by local clubs or run by a private group. These camps usually run one-week sessions (Monday–Friday) and offer morning, afternoon, evening, or morning-through-evening programs.

Day camps are often the best choice for the recreation-level player because they include social interaction, some structured activities, and learning about soccer. Perhaps the biggest downside to day camps is that your child won't get to meet players from other areas.

Overnight Camps Overnight (also called residential) camps are designed for dedicated travel-level soccer players who are between the ages of twelve and eighteen. There's a heavy emphasis on fundamental skills, tactics, and match play (both small- and full-sided). Overnight camps are for players looking for an eat-drink-breathe-sleep soccer experience.

Overnight camps can last from five days to three weeks and are usually held at boarding schools or colleges. Most of these camps offer morning and afternoon instructional sessions, followed by evening games. Nighttime events include daily review sessions with coaches, soccer videos, and social gatherings such as dances and movies.

Overnight camps usually offer lower rates to commuters—kids who opt not to stay overnight. This option will save you money while allowing your child to get most of the camp benefits.

Instructors at overnight camps usually are experienced youth, high school, or college coaches, and college—or even professional—players.

Wait Until They're Ready

A child's readiness for camp depends on the child. The amount of time a child has played is not as much a consideration as the child's maturity level. A half-day camp is usually no problem for a five- or six-year-old, while a seven- or eight-year-old could probably handle a full-day camp session.

Residential camps are usually for the more serious player—one who plays on a travel, select, or district team. Many soccer experts feel a residential camp is never a good idea for a child under nine and even then the decision to attend overnight camp should not be taken lightly. If the child is outgoing and independent, going away to camp might not be a problem. But for a shy child, day camp will be more effective and less traumatic. More often than not, children will initiate the discussion about attending an overnight camp themselves when they're ready.

Your child will have the opportunity to meet kids from all over, but won't get a lot of sleep—think of a slumber party atmosphere!

An overnight camp can be tough but rewarding. Being away from home is a great opportunity for a child to mature and meet kids from different places.

Advanced Overnight Camps After a few years of residential camp, highly skilled players may want more training. That's where advanced (often called elite) camps come in. Advanced camps are typically for travel players and up, including premier, select, and ODP players. These camps are more expensive than regular overnight camps. They take individual skill training and tactical education to the next level. Many offer special sessions on nutrition, strength training, sports psychology, and college soccer. Some require letters of recommendation. Camps like these can afford to be choosy, as there is often competition for camp openings. This type of camp is good for the passionate player.

Specialty Camps Choosing a day camp or an overnight camp isn't enough. The next thing to consider is what type of camp is best for your child. A regular camp may suffice, but you may want to consider one of the many specialty camps that are available.

Goalkeeper Camps Goalkeeper camps offer, as the name implies, specialized training for keepers. Some are run in association with a regular soccer camp. Most people feel that it's important that players under twelve develop all-around playing skills and not specialize in one position, so keeper camps are better for older kids who have decided to concentrate on the position. But if an under-twelve player who is very interested in goalkeeping is getting sufficient field time with the local team, a goalkeeper camp could be good for a few reasons:

1. It will teach the basics of the position and create a solid base to build upon, if the child decides to continue as a keeper.
2. It will teach the safe way to play the position.
3. It will give your child the chance to get together with other players who have the same passion for goalkeeping.
4. It will provide exposure to dedicated coaches in a setting designed solely for keeper development.

Some goalkeeper camps have "advanced" weeks, usually for players sixteen and up. They focus more on the strategy and psychology of the position than on fundamentals.

Striker Camps Striker camps are relatively new. Often combined with a goalkeeper camp, the emphasis in a striker camp is on shooting and scoring. Campers train in their specialty throughout the day, and then join forces in the evening to put what they've learned to the test. Goalkeeper and striker camps share certain elements. Instructors emphasize skill development, tactics, and decision making. Campers develop pride in their position. And they learn to be mentally strong. It's not easy to make an error like letting in a soft goal or missing an open net, but that's part of the game.

Girls-Only Camps Girls-only camps are a good choice for girls who are uncomfortable with competing against boys. Many girls will get more out of a camp in which they aren't distracted—or intimidated—by boys. Athletically, many girls have little trouble competing with boys until age twelve or thirteen, and often beyond. Girls twelve and over can sometimes be overshadowed on the field by boys of similar age, which is why some coaches and players prefer female-only camps. The important thing to take into account is if playing with boys will matter to your daughter.

Team Camps Sending an entire team to camp can create stronger team relationships and improve team communication. The team gets evaluated by several coaches who are knowledgeable and impartial. It's appropriate to send a high school–age team to camp. Some coaches may send teams with players as young as twelve or thirteen. It depends on whether the coach feels that the team's goals can only be accomplished in a camp setting. Most teams will improve if they get a chance to play at a higher level than they have been playing. The downside to team camps is that the team may not get as much of a "camp experience" because the players tend to stick around each other.

College Camps Some overnight camps are closely connected with college soccer programs. They're held on college campuses, run by college coaches, and staffed by players from that college's team. College camps offer some obvious advantages: extensive athletic facilities, good food, nice accommodations, and excellent staffs. They also provide a taste of the college experience, covering lots of items of interest to a high school junior or senior: SAT preparation and test-taking tips, admissions process, recruiting, NCAA rules and regulations, scholarships, and more. Plus, it's a chance for the child to see a school and develop a relationship with a college coach.

International Camps　International camps in Europe and South America offer players a chance to travel, meet players from other parts of the world, and receive instruction from foreign coaches. But they're expensive!

More Than Soccer　Some players, no matter how much they love soccer, want something else from a camp—and some camps are set up to recognize this. Campers spend part of the day learning about and playing soccer; the rest of the day they spend hiking, rafting, or doing a number of other activities.

Squaw Valley Soccer Camp in California, for instance, combines soccer with more than a dozen other activities, such as mountain biking, white-water rafting, paintball, ice skating, and indoor rock climbing. A camp like this may provide the perfect answer for the child who wants to play some soccer but try out other activities as well.

The director of Two Rivers Soccer Camp feels too much soccer can lead to burnout and a mixed program offers the best of both worlds. Two Rivers, surrounded by national forest in the Northern California Sierras, offers non-soccer activities such as archery, hiking, rafting, swimming, and fishing, as well as campfires, movies, and crafts.

Referee Camp　There aren't too many camps for youngsters who are interested in being a referee. CYSA-South's Referee Camp in southern California is a residential camp where young refs spend time in classrooms, use the knowledge they've gained to referee games, receive assessments on an individual basis, and receive emotional and practical support from reffing mentors.

How to Judge Which Camp is Best

Selecting a camp for your child should take a little more time than deciding which movie to see on a Saturday night. There are lots of things to consider:

Past Experience　Talk with former campers to find out how good the place really is; there's no substitute for personal experience. Ask about the format, the food, and the friendliness of the coaches.

Safety　This depends on the camp. While a rigorous residential camp for older players in a remote location should ideally have a medical professional in residence, a day facility for younger players, with ready

telephone access to medical personnel, might not need more than a few instructors who are certified in CPR or basic first aid. All residential camps should have a trainer certified by NATA (National Athletic Trainers Association) available twenty-four hours a day, every day.

Parents should always ask a camp director about medical personnel and then decide if they are comfortable with the staffing level. Parents also need to ask if campers have constant access to water.

Staff You're putting your trust in the camp staff, so they'd better have lots of experience with soccer, and—what's sometimes overlooked—with kids. Many people feel that a director of a soccer camp should have a master's degree in education or physical education, as well as an A license or its equivalent.

As has been noted throughout this book, youth soccer should first and foremost be about fun. With that in mind, it's most important that all coaching staff love what they are doing, love the sport, like kids, and be able to communicate their love of the sport to the children.

Another factor to consider is staff-to-camper ratio. Be sure to note the difference in adult-to-child and coach-to-child ratio; adults include all the counselors and administrators who are around and in contact with the campers, but the coach-to-camper ratio only includes those who are directly responsible for the campers' instruction. Ratios of one adult to eight campers and one coach for every ten campers are considered very good.

Philosophy What is the camp's philosophy? Are there lots of drills? Are games stressed? Is there a balance? Some camps may be trying to create the next generation of pro players, while others are devoted to developing kids with a better understanding and appreciation for the game. Check out the daily schedule in the camp brochure.

Price Unless you're a recent lottery winner, money probably is an object.

Find out what exactly you're paying for. What does the camp fee cover? Are meals included? Will your child receive a ball and shirt?

For comparison purposes, half-day "Mini Camp" programs for kids ages five through eight usually cost $100–$200 for a four- or five-day session. Some start as low as $50 for four or five 1½-hour sessions. Day camps usually range from $150–$200 per week for full-day sessions. The price goes up for players who attend residential camps as commuters (don't spend the night). Residential camps, where players sleep over, begin around $350 for the week, and can cost as much as $650 for some specialty programs, such as goalkeeper camps.

When determining camp costs, you need to ask how long the camp week actually is. Some camps that run Sunday to Friday really only offer four days of instruction. Sunday is settling-in day, and Friday is closing ceremonies and awards. Parents should ask about the schedule so they can determine if a camp is a good value.

Accommodations Will your child be playing on well-kept fields? Are there indoor facilities in case it rains? Air-conditioned lecture halls and dorm rooms are also a plus during those hot summer months.

Roommates Most camp administrators try to accommodate roommate requests, but you should make the request well in advance. Don't discount a camp just because your child can't room with a friend. Even if a pair of friends isn't placed together, they should have time to see each other during the camp day. Also, not rooming with a friend can often make it easier to make new friends.

Miscellaneous Some other things to consider include locale (how far from home is the camp?), activities (does the camp host talent shows, movies, awards ceremonies, pizza parties, and so on?), and special events (are any pro players or coaches scheduled to make a guest appearance?).

What to Bring Most camps will tell campers what to bring. Some of the items often mentioned include shorts, socks, shirts, shin guards, underwear, broken-in cleats (indoor and outdoor), sneakers, sleeping bag, bedding, towels, swimsuit, casual clothes, ball with your child's name on it, food (day programs like the kids to bring healthy snacks such as sports bars and bananas, as well as drinks), phone numbers for people to contact in an emergency, medications taken and instructions for their use, money for snacks and souvenirs, water bottle, personal hygiene needs, and books (games, cards) for free time.

Just as important is what *not* to take to most camps: radios, CD players, large amounts of money, a TV or computer, pagers or cellular phones, non-soccer sports equipment—and a soccer ball if the camp is going to be providing one.

Wrap-Up

So, is it camp time in your household? Your child is best able to answer that. If you're getting a barrage of requests to go to camp and comments about getting better, there won't be burnout. But if you're the one pushing the idea and getting the camp brochures, this might be an indication that your child has had enough. Parents must determine how important the game is to their children, how much they want to improve, and how much fun they are having before deciding to send them to camp.

For camp listings, go to *Soccer America* magazine's Web site *(www. socceramerica.com)* and go to its Soccer Camp Directory.

Soccer Tournaments

There are thousands of youth soccer tournaments staged in the United States every year—full-sided, small-sided, girls-only, small, and huge. They can be as close as the next town and as far as across the country—or across the ocean.

Every state soccer association sponsors at least one statewide soccer tournament to determine a champion in each of its age groups. Some sponsor separate tournaments for their recreation and elite teams, called the American Cup and open tournaments respectively. Most travel and premier teams will participate in state tournaments that are staged as single-elimination affairs. You play one game per week in the fall or spring (or both) until you are eliminated or are the champion.

Other tournaments are club-sponsored. They are administered by various clubs as a means of fund-raising and usually take place during a single weekend. Each team is placed in its age bracket and sometimes has a choice of a more or less competitive group in which to compete. Matches are shortened out of compassion for the kids—who sometimes need to play three matches in a day.

Elite tournaments, complete with big-time sponsors, attract "super clubs"—highly competitive teams often drawn from several towns, or even counties. Teams come to these tournaments not only to win but to perform in front of college coaches in hopes of being offered a scholarship to play at a university. These tournaments often run for an entire week. Only well-financed, high-level clubs need apply.

Young players (under thirteen years old) typically participate in local and state tournaments. As they get older and play on more competitive levels, their teams may opt for larger tournaments, some of which attract youth teams from other countries. Really ambitious teams may choose to travel overseas to an international youth tournament. See the next section of this chapter "Soccer Tours" for details.

Most youth tournaments are held during the spring and fall seasons, and they range from dozens to hundreds of teams. When choosing a first tournament for your team, wait until your players are twelve years old and begin with a small local affair—one to which you can drive without the expense of having to stay overnight in a hotel. Ask tournament administrators about the level of play you can expect. Bigger tournaments will offer you the choice of an A or B bracket within your age group, with the more competitive teams playing in the A bracket.

Listings of youth soccer tournaments are available in state and national soccer newsletters and from the *Soccer America* magazine Web site. It lists event dates, age brackets, formats, registration fees, and contact information. Be sure to start the application process early. Many tournaments fill up months prior to their start dates. You'll have to request the application forms and, if traveling out of state, do the paperwork required by your state association. Some tournaments have begun to allow coaches to register online.

Soccer Tours

Some youth soccer teams take soccer tours to other countries during their spring school vacations and the summer. Soccer tours allow kids to play in international youth soccer tournaments and to experience other cultures, languages, and foods. They are great ways to meet youth from around the world. Although trips are available for young players, most teams wait until players are between fourteen and six-teen—when they are able to appreciate cultural exchange but before they are caught up in the throes of touring and applying to colleges and the other rites of late high school.

Popular destinations include England, Sweden, Denmark, and Holland. These countries offer opportunities to play in tournaments, train with international coaches, play friendly matches with local clubs, and do plenty of sightseeing.

Various types of organizations facilitate the tours. Soccer tour companies will help you tailor your trip to your specifications. They can offer a variety of package tours to virtually anywhere in Europe, or they can work with you to put together a tour customized to your needs. You may want more soccer and less touring—or the reverse. You can choose between competitive international tournament play or friendly matches with local teams, clinics, and training sessions. Or you can put the trip together yourself with assistance from the administrators of a major tournament, such as the Gothia Cup (held every July in Gothenburg, Sweden), who can help you arrange everything except your plane tickets.

If your child's team has no desire to go on a soccer tour, there are other ways to go. Cultural exchange groups, such as People to People International, also put together soccer teams made up of individuals from around the United States.

Touring Tips

- Work with an established tour company. Specifically ask how many times the company and tour leaders have brought teams to the country or tournament in which you are interested. Lots can go wrong when traveling in groups, so don't take a chance on an organization that's still working out the bugs.
- Learn about your destination city before you arrive. Knowing about the people, climate, where the points of interest are, and security precautions will make for a more enjoyable trip. I'd also recommend investing in a small dictionary and phrase book, if for no other reason than to be able to read the menus in restaurants.
- When feasible, house responsible youth in tournament-provided hostels (usually schools) rather than hotels. Although they will most likely sleep on floors with mats (or at best on cots), the experience of mingling with teams from other countries will be invaluable.

- Adults—except for the team leader who stays with the kids in the hostel—typically stay in nearby hotels. When choosing, try to avoid hotels where youth players are staying—if you value your sleep.

- There is a wide range in prices, usually due to length of stay, accommodations selected, location of the tournaments, and so on. This makes it difficult to compare costs. A couple of things to ask about: Is the cost for the coach's travel part of the quoted per-person fee, or is it additional? Most tour compa-

nies promote their services by stating that the coach travels free, but I've spoken to parents who were surprised at the last minute to find that this simply meant that they had to take up a collection for the coach's costs.

- Meals can be pretty minimal for kids in the hostels. One American girl complained to me that they were only served bread for breakfast. This was a bit of an exaggeration—the kids were also offered hard-boiled eggs and juice—but you may want to build extra money for supplemental meals into your budget.

- Tournaments offer valuable extras to attendees, but the value varies. Ask for specifics. The Gothia Cup, for instance, offers cards that enable participants to use public transportation throughout the city and gain admission to amusement parks and museums. Other tournaments often offer less.

- Choose a tournament that will provide competitive matches for your players. This is not typically a problem for boys' teams on tour, but it can be for high-level girls' teams. Girls' soccer is not nearly as developed as boys' soccer in most of Europe and elsewhere. I've seen matches where U.S. girls' teams consistently win by double-digit margins until the final rounds—where they often find themselves pitted against other U.S. teams.

- To get a sense of the competitive level to expect, discuss the level of your team with tour company personnel or tournament administrators. If possible, talk to coaches who have attended in previous years. Bigger tournaments will have an A and B bracket from which to choose.

- Ask about the percentage of American teams in the tournament in your gender and age bracket. You probably don't want to travel thousands of miles to play mostly other American teams.

CHAPTER 12

Soccer Around the World

Pelé, the greatest player of all time, refers to soccer as "the beautiful game." It unites people of all ages, colors, creeds, religions, and social backgrounds. A man in London and a young girl in Indonesia may share the same passion for "the beautiful game." But why?

Perhaps it's the game's simplicity. Got a round object? That's pretty much all you need to get rolling. No need for a lot of fancy equipment. Somewhere in the world at this very moment, kids of all abilities are kicking a tennis ball or a bundle of rolled-up socks and playing an informal version of the same game that is played in front of more than 100,000 fans at major stadiums around the world.

The popularity of the sport has come a long way in 150 years. There are more than 250 million registered participants from Algeria to Zimbabwe. Soccer is a multibillion-dollar global industry, with top players worth millions of dollars.

The game stirs immeasurable emotions in its most diehard followers. Many fans ask their loved ones to spread their burial ashes on the field of their favorite club after they die. At the English club Everton, for example, this ritual reportedly occurs an average of six times a week!

The United States is finally being swept up in the passion that has long captivated the rest of the world. Soccer was brought to America by English settlers in the 1800s. An early form of soccer was popular in colleges and universities until it was replaced by rugby, which grew into American football. While American football became more popular, soccer remained rooted in cities with large immigrant populations. A large number of European immigrants came to America in the early

1900s. They played soccer on city streets and playgrounds, though it still didn't capture the nation's imagination.

It didn't help matters that the U.S. Men's National Team, after shocking mighty England in the 1950 World Cup, had a forty-year dry spell without a single World Cup appearance. But the U.S. men played in all three World Cups in the '90s and hosted the 1994 tournament. The 1994 World Cup was a benchmark for the expansion and development of the game in this country; it was the impetus for Major League Soccer, the first-division U.S. professional league.

The profile of the world's most popular sport was raised even further in the United States thanks to the incredible success of the U.S. Women's Team. The women's success at the 1996 Olympics and 1999 Women's World Cup were major factors in the development of the Women's United Soccer Association (WUSA), a first-division pro league. After a debut in spring 2001 and several exciting seasons, the league suspended operation. It hopes to return to action in the near future.

The number of people playing "the beautiful game" midway through the first decade of the twenty-first century is slightly lower than it was at the turn of the century, but it is still near an all-time high. According to SGMA Internationals latest Sports Participation Topline Report, 15.9 million people in the United States played soccer at least once in 2004, a 3.3 percent increase since 1987. Of that total, 11.1 million, or almost three out of every four, were under the age of eighteen. Almost 700,000 boys and girls participated in high school soccer during the 2003 to 2004 school year, a whopping 100 percent increase since 1989.

The numbers are just as promising at the next level. Collegiate varsity teams outnumber American football teams. There were 619 NCAA gridiron football programs in 2002–03, a number far below the 732 NCAA men's teams (202 in Division I) and 879 NCAA women's teams (288 in Division I). As the sport of soccer enjoys unequaled success in the United States and around the world, it's worth taking a moment to find out where the game began.

Soccer History

Soccer, known to Europe and most of the rest of the world as football, developed in England in the mid-nineteenth century. But no one knows for sure when and where a round object was first kicked around in a gamelike atmosphere.

It's almost impossible to pin down the precise origin of soccer, although it most likely derived from a combination of ancient games, including *tsu chu* (China), *kemari* (Japan), *episkyros* (Greece), *harpastum* (Rome), and *calcio* (Italy). *Tsu chu*, which means "kicking a ball with the foot," was played by the Chinese 2,500 years ago. As early as the mid-seventh century, the Japanese tried to kick the *mari*, a ball made of deerskin, between two bamboo shoots during *kemari* contests. They did this for exercise and as a way for different classes of people to play and relax together.

Native Americans were playing a game resembling soccer as early as the 1620s. When the Pilgrims arrived at Plymouth Rock, they found them playing a game called *pasuckquakkohowog*, which means "they gather to play football."

The English had been playing games similar to soccer for about a thousand years. Many early games were disorganized, violent, and rowdy affairs. In the early 1800s, a number of versions of soccer were being played in private schools throughout England. Some allowed players to use their hands; others did not. It was nearly impossible for different schools to play each other because teams couldn't agree on the rules. In 1848, students from Cambridge University created the first rules. The Cambridge Rules formed the basis for the Laws of the Game. Organized soccer began in October 1863, when the English Football Association was founded in London. By the end of the year, the game split into two games, rugby and association football (soccer). Rugby, which allowed players to use their hands, gave rise to American and Australian football. Soccer became popular in the rest of the world.

English explorers, settlers, traders, and tourists shared their game in their world travels. The game spread all over Europe, to South America, and to the United States in the latter half of the 1800s. (The first organized soccer team in the United States was the Oneida Football Club of Boston. It was formed in 1862 and stopped operating in 1865 after three undefeated seasons. It is the oldest club outside England.) By the beginning of the twentieth century, soccer was being played in most countries.

So where did the term *soccer* come from? "Association football" was a long name, so college students in England began calling the game *assoc*. The name was further shortened to *soc*, and eventually became soccer.

As soccer developed throughout the world, teams were playing against each other, and the need for proper organization grew. On May 21, 1904, the Fédération Internationale de Football Association (FIFA) was formed by representatives from Belgium, Denmark, France, Holland, Spain, Sweden, and Switzerland, to "promote the game of association football."

FIFA   FIFA, the international governing body of soccer, rules international soccer. FIFA updates the rules of the game and ensures that they are properly applied, promotes the sport at all levels, and runs all worldwide soccer competitions, including the World Cup, the sport's ultimate event. FIFA organizes administrative, coaching, refereeing, and sports medicine training courses. It also governs pro players transferring from one nation to another. FIFA's headquarters are in Zurich, Switzerland.

FIFA has 204 member nations—more than the United Nations!—divided into confederations representing five continents and the Oceania region (Australia, New Zealand, and other South Pacific island nations). The United States joined FIFA in 1913.

The World Cup   Since the first international match was played between England and Scotland in 1872, the most important soccer games have been those played between teams that represent their countries. Each nation gathers its best players and forms a "national team." These teams play each other often and take part in international tournaments.

There are countless tournaments at the international and club level all over the world. The European Championship, held every four years, determines the top European national team. The Copa America, South America's national-team championship, is held every two years, as is the African Nations Cup. For a soccer player, nothing beats lifting a championship trophy in front of thousands of adoring fans.

The trophy most sought after is the World Cup. Forget about the Super Bowl or the World Series; the World Cup, soccer's world championship tournament, is *the* most important sporting event on earth. It is a showcase for the greatest national teams and the world's best players. Every player dreams of participating in the World Cup.

World Cup time is almost a national holiday in many parts of the world. Entire countries practically shut down when their teams are playing in the tournament. Schools and businesses often close on game day. Victories are often greeted with wild celebrations and all-night street parties. Entire nations go into despair after defeats.

The passion that is generated by the World Cup is almost indescribable. Consider this: Colombian defender Andres Escobar was shot dead outside a Colombian bar on July 2, 1994. Why? Because he scored an own goal in a 2–1 World Cup loss to the United States.

Played every four years since 1930 (except 1942 and 1946 because of World War II), the World Cup attracts nearly every soccer-playing nation to its qualifying stage. A record 198 countries entered qualifying competition for the 2002 World Cup, which was co-hosted by Japan and

South Korea. The next World Cup will be played in Germany during the summer of 2006. Many nations will have to play dozens of games over the course of almost two years just to qualify for the 2006 World Cup.

But it's worth the effort. Hundreds of thousands of fans attend World Cup matches, and billions more watch on television. The champion has worldwide bragging rights for the next four years. (Four-time champion Brazil has won the most World Cups. The United States has never won.) Often, reputations are made and new stars emerge on soccer's grandest stage. Of course, a poor performance can make a career take a turn for the worse. That's what makes the World Cup so special.

Superstars, Yesterday and Today

Every sport has its list of superstars. Baseball has Babe Ruth and Willie Mays. Basketball has Michael Jordan and Wilt Chamberlain. Hockey has Wayne Gretzky and Bobby Orr. Football has Joe Montana and Walter Payton. In soccer, Brazil's Pelé is at the top of the list.

Edson Arantes do Nascimento, known simply as Pelé, is the most famous name in sports. His skill, creativity, and strength mesmerized defenders—and fans.

Pelé played his best in his biggest games. He won three World Cup championships with Brazil. He scored his first World Cup goal in 1958 at age seventeen. He scored twice in Brazil's 5–2 win over Sweden in the 1958 final. In all, he won three World Cups (1958, 1962, and 1970) and scored 1,281 goals in 1,363 games.

Pelé joined the New York Cosmos of the now-defunct North American Soccer League in 1975 and played until 1977. His brief NASL career helped spark an interest in the league and establish the popularity of soccer in the United States. Pelé single-handedly established soccer as a grassroots American sport.

Still need proof of his popularity? In Africa in 1967, a civil war was raging between the Nigerian government and its rebelling province of Biafra. The two sides agreed to stop the fighting for three days because Pelé was in the region with his club team, Santos, to play a pair of exhibition matches. After Pelé left, the truce ended and war resumed.

Pelé may be soccer's greatest player ever, but the sport has seen its fair share of superstar athletes through the years. Here are some of them:

- **Roberto Baggio** (Italy). Baggio, an Italian national-team star in the '80s and '90s, was the European Player of the Year in 1993 and the FIFA World Player of the Year in 1995. Unfortunately, he's best remembered for missing the final penalty kick in the 1994 World Cup final against Brazil.

- **Gordon Banks** (England). Banks was probably the best goal-keeper ever. He made what is considered the world's greatest save, deflecting a Pelé header over the crossbar in the 1970 World Cup. Banks won the 1966 World Cup, but his career came to a premature end when he lost an eye in a car crash.
- **Franz Beckenbauer** (Germany). Beckenbauer captained West Germany to the World Cup title in 1974 and was the winning coach in the 1990 World Cup. The two-time European Player of the Year is credited with creating the attacking sweeper role in the late '60s. Beckenbauer, who won three titles in five years with the Cosmos (NASL), was nicknamed "the Kaiser" for his leadership abilities.
- **George Best** (Northern Ireland). At his peak in the latter half of the '60s, Best was a superb dribbler and an outstanding finisher. He was one of the first big-name international stars to sign with the NASL, and he played six years in the league (1976–1981). Best was named European Player of the Year in 1968.
- **Bobby Charlton** (England). Perhaps England's most famous player, Charlton is the top English national-team scorer. Best had a powerful shot; many of his best goals came from long range.
- **Johan Cruyff** (Netherlands). Cruyff, the greatest Dutch player of all time, had outstanding ball control. The three-time European Player of the Year won three straight European Cups with the Dutch club Ajax in the early '70s. Cruyff captained Holland in the 1974 World Cup (his team lost to West Germany in the final) and later played for three years in the NASL.
- **Alfredo Di Stefano** (Spain). Di Stefano, a two-time European Player of the Year, was the Spanish star of the '50s and '60s. He led his club, Real Madrid, to the title in the first five European Cups.
- **Eusebio** (Portugal). Eusebio was the first African superstar; he grew up in Mozambique, which was then still one of Portugal's African colonies. Eusebio, the 1965 European Player of the Year, was the top scorer in the 1966 World Cup. He won seven Portuguese club titles with Benfica before ending his career in the NASL.
- **Diego Maradona** (Argentina). Small and powerful, Maradona was the best player in the world throughout the '80s and early '90s. His great ball control allowed him to weave through defenders.

He captained Argentina to the 1986 World Cup title and was named the tournament's MVP. His career was cut short by numerous drug problems.

- **Bobby Moore** (England). Moore was one of the greatest defenders ever. He captained England to the 1966 World Cup title. A great team leader, Moore played in more than a hundred games with England's national team. He died from cancer in 1993.
- **Michel Platini** (France). Platini, the midfield general of French teams in the mid-'80s, is the only player to win three straight European Player of the Year awards (1983–1985). He won the European Championship in 1984 and was the top scorer of the tournament.
- **Lev Yashin** (Soviet Union). Yashin is the only goalkeeper to be named European Player of the Year (1963). He won an Olympic gold medal in 1956. With his incredible reflexes and agility, Yashin was able to stop shots other keepers couldn't even reach.

Who are some of the most recognizable stars of recent years? Learn a little about the following players, and you'll amaze the toughest critics: your kids!

- **Freddy Adu** (Ghana/U.S.). Played his first international match with the US U-17 National Team at 13 years old. Today he plays for DC United of Major League Soccer. Expect to hear a lot more of him in the future.
- **Gabriel Batistuta** (Argentina). Dynamite goal scorer. Top scorer when Argentina won the 1991 Copa America. One of the top players in the 1994 and 1998 World Cups.
- **David Beckham** (England). One of the world's best crossers. Powerful shot. Married to Victoria Adams of the Spice Girls.
- **Dennis Bergkamp** (Netherlands). All-time leading scorer for the Dutch national team.
- **Thierry Henry** (France). A complete player who is lethal in front of the net, Henry was the top scorer in the English Premier League (22 goals) while playing for Arsenal. He was a member of France's victorious World Cup (1998), European Champion (2000) and Confederation's Cup (2003) teams.
- **Michael Owen** (England). The next English superstar. The youngest player ever to start for England. Scored two goals at the 1998 World Cup as an eighteen-year-old.
- **Raul** (Spain). Spanish soccer sensation of the latter half of the '90s.

- **Ronaldinho Gaucho** (Brazil). One of the world's most creative attacking players, Ronaldinho was a member of Brazil's victorious World Cup (2002) and Confederation's Cup (2005) teams. He was also voted FIFA World Player of the Year in 2004.
- **Ronaldo** (Brazil). Marvelous goal scorer. FIFA World Player of the Year in 1996 and 1997—the first player to win award twice. Voted best player at the 1998 World Cup.
- **Alan Shearer** (England). Prolific goal scorer. Youngest player (at 17 years, 240 days) to score three goals in a Premier League game.
- **Andriy Shevchenko** (Ukraine). A star with AC Milan in the Italian Series A, Shevchenko is a freekick artist and good both on the finish and assist. In 2004 he was voted the European Footballer of the Year (Ballon d' Or).
- **Zinedine Zidane** (France). One of the world's best players. Dynamic dribbler and creator. Scored two goals in 3–0 win over Brazil in the 1998 World Cup final. Led France to victory at the 2000 European Championship.

Most of a soccer player's career is spent with a club team. Countries all over the world have professional leagues. Soccer-crazy countries like England and Germany have several pro leagues. Players do not have to play in a league in their own country. U.S. native Claudio Reyna, for example, plays for a club called Glasgow Rangers in Scotland.

Because professional soccer is a relatively recent U.S. game, the list of great U.S. players isn't too long. The first soccer stars in the U.S. were actually foreign players who joined the North American Soccer League. The NASL was formed in 1967 in large part because of the success of the 1966 World Cup in England. Investors were attracted by the large crowds attending games in other parts of the world. Also, it was believed pro soccer teams could fill seats at stadiums on days that baseball teams were out of town. Pelé was the star of the NASL. Other NASL players who helped popularize the game in America were George Best, Gordon Banks, and Franz Beckenbauer. The NASL collapsed in 1985.

Major League Soccer, the U.S. Division I outdoor professional league that was launched in 1996 with ten teams, has provided a "home" league for U.S. players. Today, young fans can follow the MLS careers of such U.S. players as Mike Petke, Frankie Hejduk, Landon Donovan, and Freddy Adu. And, like the NASL, the MLS has also attracted stars from other countries. Some of the top foreigners in Major League Soccer include Youri Djorkaeff (France), Amado Guevara (Honduras) and Carlos Ruiz (Guatemala). Twelve teams participated in the summer league's tenth season in 2005. Teams play thirty-two regular-season games. The playoffs culminate in the MLS Cup, the league's one-game championship.

Just ten years ago, it's a good bet most people couldn't name a single professional soccer player in the United States. Today, Landon Donovan and company are everywhere: endorsing sports drinks on TV commercials, hawking the latest soccer gear on billboards, and making guest appearances on TV shows.

But it's not only the men who are beginning to get our attention.

Women's Soccer

Chances are good that you've heard of U.S. soccer player Mia Hamm. Hamm is one of more than 30 million women in more than eighty-five countries who play soccer.

Soccer started as a "man's game" and was considered too demanding for women. Girls were discouraged from playing soccer—and most other sports, for that matter—because they were believed to be too delicate. During World War I, women started to work in factories because the men were off fighting. As women gained a place in the workforce, they also gained a place on the soccer field.

The most famous of the early women's teams was England's Dick, Kerr Ladies. In 1920 the Dick, Kerr Ladies were hugely popular and played in front of crowds of up to 53,000. But the English men's soccer association, which owned most of the soccer stadiums, banned women from using their fields, thus slowing down the development of the women's game in England. Still, women's soccer continued to grow in Europe and America.

In the early '70s in America, youth soccer was taking off at the same time that more opportunities for girls were arising. Title IX is credited with spurring the growth of women's athletics, particularly soccer, in high schools and colleges.

Title IX is the federal law passed in 1972 mandating equal opportunities for females in educational, government-funded programs. After the law was passed, high schools and colleges around the country started developing girls' sports teams. This encouraged more and more girls to become athletes. Disparities between sports opportunities for males and females still exist, but conditions have improved since the law was passed.

The number of female players is exploding at every level, from youth teams through high school and college. According to SICA's 1999 National Soccer Participation Survey, 7.5 million girls under eighteen played soccer in 1998. That number represented 41.2 percent of all youth players and a 24 percent increase among female players since 1987.

The numbers are just as promising at the college level. In 1981, the first year the NCAA kept records in women's soccer, there were 80 teams in Divisions I, II, and III. By 1990, that number had reached 318. During the 1999–2000 NCAA soccer season, the number had grown to 879, an astronomical 999 percent increase in less than twenty years.

The W-League, the highest level of competitive soccer for women in the United States outside of college or national-team programs, was officially introduced in 1995 after a successful trial run during the summer of 1994. In 1998 the women's league was divided into two levels, forming W-1 (elite) and W-2 divisions. Classified as an "open" league, the W-League allows college, amateur, and youth players to play alongside professionals at a high level. It is a place for women's college soccer players to prepare for their upcoming seasons and for former college players to play after their collegiate careers are over. Players with W-League experience include 1999 Women's World Cup veterans Michelle Akers, Mia Hamm, Kristine Lilly, Julie Foudy, Brandi Chastain, Carla Overbeck, Sara Whalen, and Briana Scurry.

The most popular soccer team in the United States is the U.S. Women's National Team. Just over ten years ago, the women's team played games in front of "crowds" of a hundred fans. When the team started in 1985, players and coaches had to sew the "USA" letters on their own uniforms. When the U.S. squad came back from winning the first FIFA Women's World Championship (held in China in 1991), it was greeted only by friends, family, and one journalist. Most U.S. papers and TV stations didn't even mention it.

The media began to sense the impact of the U.S. Women's National Team in 1996. That year, the U.S. team's Olympic gold-medal victory over China brought the women respect and recognition. People who didn't follow soccer—or any sport—could relate to a gold medal.

The popularity of women's soccer reached new heights three years after the U.S. gold-medal performance.

The biggest blockbuster during the summer of 1999 was not the newest *Star Wars* movie. It was the U.S. Women's National Team, which defeated China on penalty kicks to win the Women's World Cup. The tournament captured the attention of the world. More than 650,000 fans went to the thirty-two matches across the United States, shattering attendance records for a women's sporting event. More than a billion people watched worldwide on television. Forty million people—the biggest U.S. TV audience ever to watch a soccer game—tuned in to the final. The Women's World Cup was the biggest and most successful women's sporting event in history. Much of America fell in love with soccer for the first time.

The victorious U.S. women thrilled the entire nation and became the story of the year. The incredible TV and print exposure the team received was a far cry from the coverage it got just eight years earlier. According to the U.S. Soccer Media Guide, the U.S. Women's National Team "went from America's best-kept secret to an American pop icon." The players were seen almost daily on ESPN's *SportsCenter*. They were on the covers of *Time*, *Newsweek*, *Sports Illustrated*, and *People* magazines. The members of the team became celebrities, making appearances at Disneyland, the White House, and on *Late Show with David Letterman*.

More important, the members of the U.S. team became heroes to young fans. Players like Mia Hamm, Julie Foudy, and Kristine Lilly became positive role models for younger generations of female players.

The next generation of female stars is being born on soccer fields across America. Girls in the United States have all kinds of opportunities: they can play soccer in high school, watch their favorite soccer stars on television, get a soccer scholarship for college, and even represent their country in the Olympics. As the twenty-first century begins, interest in women's soccer all over the globe is at an all-time high. In places as diverse as Thailand and the island of Martinique, women are falling in love with the game.

FIFA president Joseph "Sepp" Blatter may have said it best during the 1999 Women's World Cup: "The future of football is feminine."

The Laws of the Game

The rules of soccer haven't changed much since they were originally created in 1863. The sport is broken down into seventeen laws, which are discussed here in an abbreviated format. For a complete set of the Laws of the Game, check *www.fifa.com* on the Internet.

Law 1: The Field of Play The soccer field is rectangular, with a width of 70 to 80 yards and a length of 110 to 120 yards. The two longer boundary lines are called touchlines. The two shorter lines are called goal lines. A halfway line divides the field equally in two. At each end of the field is a goal area, a penalty area, and a securely anchored goal that is 24 feet wide and 8 feet high. Corner arcs and flag posts are in each corner of the field.

Law 2: The Ball The ball must be spherical with a circumference of 27 to 28 inches and a weight of 14 to 16 ounces. The referee will stop the match to replace a defective ball.

Law 3: The Number of Players A match is played by two teams of eleven players each, including the goalkeeper. A match may not start if either team has fewer than seven players. Up to three substitutions may be made in an official match. A substitute may only enter the field of play after receiving a signal from the referee.

Law 4: The Players' Equipment The basic equipment consists of a jersey, shorts, stockings, shin guards, and footwear. The shin guards must be covered entirely by the stockings. Players may not wear anything, such as jewelry, that could be dangerous to themselves or each other. Goalkeepers must wear colors that distinguish them from the other players, the referee, and the assistant referees.

Law 5: The Referee The referee controls the match and has full authority. Some of the referee's duties include enforcing the Laws of the Game, acting as official timekeeper, stopping the match because of outside interference or a serious injury, ensuring that a bleeding player leaves the field of play, and restarting the match after it has been stopped. The decisions of the referee are final.

Law 6: The Assistant Referees Two assistant referees indicate when the ball has gone out of bounds, which team is entitled to a corner kick, throw-in, or goal kick, when a player is in an offside position, when a substitution is requested, and when misconduct or anything else has occurred out of the view of the referee.

Law 7: The Duration of the Match The match lasts two equal periods of forty-five minutes, unless otherwise agreed between the referee and both teams before the start of play. Players are entitled to a halftime interval of no more than fifteen minutes. The referee allows for time lost through substitutions, injuries, or any other cause. Additional time is allowed for a penalty kick to be taken at the end of each half.

Law 8: The Start and Restart of Play The winner of a coin toss decides which goal it will attack in the first half. The other team takes the kickoff to start the game. Kickoffs are also used to restart play after a goal has been scored. A dropped ball is a way of restarting a match after a temporary stoppage. The referee drops the ball at the site where the play was stopped. The play restarts when the ball touches the ground.

Law 9: The Ball In and Out of Play The ball is out of play when it has entirely crossed the goal line or touchline on the ground or in the air, or when the referee has stopped play. The ball is in play at all other times.

Law 10: The Method of Scoring A goal is scored when the entire ball crosses the line between the goalposts. The team that scores the most goals wins. If an equal number of goals are scored, the game is a tie. Some matches use overtime to break ties.

Law 11: Offside A player is in an offside position if he is closer to his opponents' goal than both the ball and two opposing players at the moment the ball is played by a teammate. Exceptions: Players are not offside if on their own half of the field, or on the opponents' half but either level with the last defender or receiving the ball directly from a goal kick, throw-in, or corner kick. A player is only penalized for being in an offside position if the referee believes the player was gaining an unfair advantage or interfering with play or with an opponent. An indirect free kick is awarded to the opposing team when a player is offside.

Law 12: Fouls and Misconduct A direct free kick is awarded to the opposing team at the spot of the foul for any of the following offenses:

- Kicking or attempting to kick an opponent
- Tripping or attempting to trip an opponent
- Jumping at an opponent
- Charging an opponent
- Striking or attempting to strike an opponent
- Pushing an opponent
- Making contact with the opponent before touching the ball while attempting to tackle the opponent
- Holding an opponent
- Spitting at an opponent
- Deliberately handling the ball (except for the goalkeeper in the penalty area)

A penalty kick is awarded if any of the above offenses are committed by players in their own penalty area.

An indirect free kick is awarded at the spot of the foul for the following offenses:

- Playing in a dangerous manner
- Obstructing an opponent
- Preventing the goalkeeper from letting go of the ball
- (As goalkeeper) Failing to release the ball within six seconds
- (As goalkeeper) Touching the ball with a hand after releasing it and before it's touched by another player
- (As goalkeeper) Touching the ball with a hand when receiving it from a teammate's kick
- (As goalkeeper) Touching the ball with a hand when receiving it directly from a teammate's throw-in

A caution (yellow card) is issued to a player who commits any of the following offenses:

- Unsporting behavior
- Dissent by word or action
- Persistent infringement of the Laws of the Game
- Delay of restart of play
- Failure to respect required distance during corner kick or free kick
- Entering or reentering field of play without the referee's permission
- Leaving the field of play without the referee's permission

An ejection (red card) is issued to a player who commits any of the following offenses:

- Serious foul play
- Violent conduct
- Spitting at any person
- Denying a goal-scoring opportunity by deliberately handling the ball
- Denying a goal-scoring opportunity by using an offense punishable by a free kick or a penalty kick
- Offensive, insulting, or abusive language
- A second caution (yellow card)

Law 13: Free Kicks Free kicks are either direct or indirect. The ball must be stationary when the kick is taken, and the kicker cannot touch the ball a second time until it has touched another player. A direct free kick can be kicked directly into the goal without touching another player first. An indirect free kick must touch another player before it enters the goal. Unless standing on their own goal line between the goalposts, the opposing team must be at least 10 yards away during a free kick. Opponents must be outside the penalty area and at least 10 yards away from players taking a free kick in their own penalty area.

Law 14: The Penalty Kick A penalty kick is awarded against a team that commits an offense that warrants a direct free kick inside its own penalty area. Additional time is allowed for a penalty kick to be taken at the end of each half or at the end of an extra period. The kick is taken from the penalty spot by a kicker who has been identified by the referee. The goalkeeper must remain on the goal line until the ball is kicked. All other players must stand at least 10 yards from the penalty spot and be outside the penalty area. The kicker may not play the ball a second time until it touches another player.

Law 15: The Throw-in A throw-in is a method of restarting play when the ball crosses the touchline on the ground or in the air. The opponents of the player who last touched the ball take the throw-in from the point where it crossed the touchline. The ball is in play immediately when it enters the field of play. The thrower may not touch the ball again until it has touched another player. A goal cannot be scored directly from a throw-in.

Law 16: The Goal Kick The goal kick is a method of restarting play when the ball, last touched by the attacking team, crosses the goal line on the ground or in the air. A defending player kicks the ball from anywhere within the goal area. All opponents must remain outside the penalty area until the ball is in play. The ball is in play when it is beyond the penalty area. The kicker cannot play the ball again until another player touches it. A goal may be scored directly from a goal kick.

Law 17: The Corner Kick The corner kick is a method of restarting play when the ball, last touched by the defending team, crosses the goal line on the ground or in the air. An attacking player kicks the ball from inside the nearest corner arc. All opponents must remain at least 10 yards from the ball until it is in play. The ball is in play when it is kicked and moves. The kicker cannot play the ball again until another player touches it. A goal may be scored directly from a corner kick.

Organizations

American Youth Soccer Organization (AYSO)

12501 South Isis Avenue
Hawthorne, CA 90250
Phone: 800–USA–AYSO, 310–643–6455
Fax: 310–643–5310
www.soccer.org

An independent nationwide organization with a registration of more than 630,000 youth ages four and a half through eighteen. AYSO stresses participation by all its members; its motto is "Everybody plays." Every effort is made to balance teams, so there are fewer lopsided games. AYSO's Very Important Person program allows children with Down's syndrome, impaired sight or hearing, autism, and similar problems to play. AYSO relies on volunteers at the community level to maintain the programs.

Fédération Internationale de Football Association (FIFA)

P.O. Box 85
8030 Zurich, Switzerland
Phone: 011–411–384–9595
Fax: 011–411–384–9696
www.fifa.com

Founded in 1904, this international governing body of soccer has 204 member nations. FIFA administers and markets all worldwide soccer competitions, including the World Cup, and also governs all soccer rule changes.

Major Indoor Soccer League

1175 Post Road East
Westport, CT 06880
Phone: 203–222–4900
Fax: 203–221–7300

The top indoor soccer league in the U.S., the MISL season runs from October to April. Seven teams will compete in the 2005 to 2006 season.

Major League Soccer

110 East 42nd Street, Suite 1000
10th Floor
New York, NY 10017
Phone: 212–450–1200
Fax: 212–450–1325
www.mlsnet.com

The only Division I professional outdoor league in the United States. Twelve teams participated in the summer league's tenth season in 2005. Teams play thirty-two regular-season games. The playoffs culminate in the MLS Cup, the league's one-game championship.

National Alliance for Youth Sports

2050 Vista Parkway
West Palm Beach, FL 33411
Phone: 800–729–2057, 561–684–1141
Fax: 561–684–2546
www.nays.org

The goal of the National Alliance for Youth Sports is to make sports safe, positive, and fun for America's youth. The nonprofit organization believes that participation in youth sports develops important character traits and values, and that the lives of youths can be positively influenced if the adults caring for them have proper training and information.

National Federation of State High School Associations (NFHS)

P.O. Box 690
Indianapolis, IN 46206
Phone: 317–972–6900
Fax: 317–822–5700
www.nfhs.org

The NFHS is a national service and administration organization of high school athletics. The mission of the NFHS is to serve its members and its related professional groups by providing leadership and national coordination for the administration of interscholastic activities that will enhance the educational experiences of high school students. The NFHS promotes participation and sports-manship to develop good citizens through interscholastic activities.

National Soccer Coaches Association of America (NSCAA)

6700 Squibb Road
Suite 215
Mission, KS 66202
Phone: 800–458–0678, 913–362–1747
Fax: 913–362–3439
www.nscaa.com

The largest single-sport coaching organization in the United States, with more than 15,000 members. Founded in 1941, the NSCAA provides educational clinics, academies, and seminars to youth, high school, college, and pro coaches. It also offers diploma courses in all fifty states. The NSCAA is dedicated to promoting soccer and to the education of coaches.

National Soccer Hall of Fame
18 Stadium Circle
Oneonta, NY 13820
Phone: 607–432–3351
Fax: 607–432–8429
www.soccerhall.org

The National Soccer Hall of Fame, established in 1979, is committed to preserving and promoting the history and sport of soccer in the United States. The Hall of Fame is on the Wright Soccer Campus, and it includes the Kicks Zone (an interactive games area), museum (with lots of old pictures, films, and memorabilia), administrative offices, outdoor fields, Kicks Hall of Fame store, and a library. The Hall of Fame is open seven days a week except for major holidays.

Soccer Association for Youth (SAY)
One North Commerce Park Drive
Suite 306-320
Cincinnati, OH 45215
Phone: 800–233–7291, 513–769–3800
Fax: 513–769–0500
www.saysoccer.org

An independent regional youth soccer organization located mainly in the Midwest, SAY's objective is maximum participation with even competition at various age levels. It serves more than 100,000 members and includes players ages four through eighteen. SAY is a national affiliate member of the U.S. Soccer Federation.

Soccer in the Streets (SITS)
2323 Perimeter Park Drive NE
Atlanta, GA 30341
Phone: 678–992–2113
www.sits.org

A national inner-city youth soccer and education program founded in 1989, SITS has implemented programs in more than fifty U.S. cities. It is an independent national organization that creates introductory programs geared toward enhancing self-esteem and life skills, with soccer as its foundation. SITS aims to build leadership in urban youth; its motto is "Let's kick drugs and crime out of our communities."

United Soccer Leagues
14497 North Dale Mabry Hwy.
Suite 201
Tampa, FL 33618
Phone: 813–963–3909
Fax: 813–963–3807
www.uslsoccer.com

The development system for soccer in the United States, similar to the minor-league system in baseball. The USL consists of the A-League (Division II), D3 Pro League (Division III), Premier Developmental League (amateur), W-League (women), and Y-League (youth). The USL serves as the official development system for Major League Soccer.

US Club Soccer

716 8th Avenue North
Myrtle Beach, SC 29577
Phone: 843–429–0006
Fax: 843–626–4681
www.usclubsoccer.com

A federation of soccer clubs founded on the belief that competitive teams and elite players need their own organization—and fewer restrictions. Unlike U.S. Youth Soccer, for example, US Club Soccer players are allowed to "play up" in age, and travel permissions are not required to attend events in other states.

U.S. Soccer Federation (USSF)

1801 South Prairie Avenue
Chicago, IL 60616
Phone: 312–808–1300
Fax: 312–808–1301
www.ussoccer.com

National governing body of American soccer. U.S. Soccer, which is directly linked to FIFA, has exclusive governing power over most domestic soccer matters. Programs under its umbrella include the administration and marketing of the U.S. national teams (men's, women's, Olympic, and youth), U.S. coaching, and refereeing development.

U.S. Youth Soccer Association (USYSA)

1717 Firman Drive, Suite 900
Richardson, TX 75081
Phone: 800–4–SOCCER, 972–235–4499
Fax: 972–235–4480
www.youthsoccer.org

The largest youth soccer service organization in the nation, with a registration of more than 3 million players. USYSA develops and administers recreational and competitive programs for kids ages five through nineteen and also runs the ODP program, which identifies and develops top youth talent. Fifty-five state associations are directly affiliated with the USYSA.

Resources

Magazines

Soccer America
P.O. Box 23704
1144 65th Street, Suite F
Oakland, CA 94623
800–997–6223 to subscribe;
    510–420–3640
Fax: 510–420–3655
Subscription: One year (20 issues)
    for $79
www.socceramerica.com

A magazine for soccer fans that
focuses on international, professional,
and college soccer—the best source
for youth tournament and camp listings. A subscription includes the
Soccer America Yellow Pages, an
annual directory of youth organizations, tournaments, camps, products, and more.

Soccer Journal
NSCAA
6700 Squib Road
Suite 215
Mission, KS 66202
Phone: 800–458–0678
Subscription: Free for NSCAA members;
    youth coach membership is $50
www.nscaa.com

The official publication of the
National Soccer Coaches Association
of America. Filled with technical
and tactical articles for high-level
coaches as well as soccer news,
Soccer Journal is published eight
times a year.

Striker
1115 Broadway, 8th Floor
New York, NY 10010
Phone: 212–807–7100
Fax: 212–620–7787
www.striker-magazine.com

Launched as a quarterly in 2005, *Striker* magazine hopes to succeed where many (*Soccer Jr.*, *Soccer Magazine*, *Soccer For Kids*, *Soccer Digest*, to name a few) did not. Look for lots of features about star players and columns with training tips and equipment reviews.

Women's Soccer World Online
1728 Mulberry Street
Montgomery, AL 36106
Phone: 334–263–0080
Single copy: $2.95
Subscription: One year (six issues) for $15
www.womensoccer.com

This online magazine is devoted to worldwide coverage of women's soccer. Offers news about all aspects of the women's game played around the world. Links to *Girls Soccer World*, an online magazine devoted to worldwide cover of girl's soccer.

World Soccer
King's Reach Tower
Stamford Street
London, England SE1 9LS
Phone: 011–44–181–888–313–5528
Single copy: $5.45
Subscription: One year (thirteen issues) for $81.00
www.worldsoccer.com

Detailed coverage of foreign leagues, teams, stars, and competitions, with an emphasis on Europe. Good source for rosters, results, and transactions.

Books

All-American Girls: The U.S. Women's National Soccer Team by Marla Miller, 221 pages, $4.99, Pocket Books (1999)

Loads of facts, quotes, and stories about members of the 1999 Women's World Cup team; gives readers real insight into the personalities of the players.

Cobi Jones Soccer Games by Cobi Jones and Andrew Gutelle, 103 pages, $16.95, Workman Publishing (1998)

A nicely designed book of tips on basic skills and fun games to play in the backyard or at the park. Perfect for youth players up to twelve or thirteen years old. The games and the tips are really good. You can tell that Jones—one of soccer's most popular players—was involved in writing the book. It comes with a size 4 practice ball.

The Complete Encyclopedia of Soccer by Keir Radnedge, 647 pages, $39.95, Carlton Books (1999)

A definitive reference book with in-depth information on national teams, international tournaments, and club competitions. Includes biographies of more than 500 of the world's greatest players of all time.

The Game and the Glory (Youth Edition) by Michelle Akers with Gregg Lewis, 187 pages, $7.99, Zonderkidz (2000)

U.S. Women's National Team veteran Michelle Akers shares the story of her life on and off the soccer field. Includes anecdotes about her teammates, her personal struggles, her battle with a disease, and her faith.

The Girls of Summer: The U.S. Women's Soccer Team and How It Changed the World by Jere Longman, $14, First Perennial (2001)

The story of how the U.S women's soccer program rose from international obscurity in the mid-1980s to win an epic World Cup battle in 1999.

Goal! The Ultimate Guide for Soccer Moms and Dads by Gloria Averbuch and Ashley Michael Hammond, 224 pages, $15.95, Rodale Press (1999)

One of the best introductions to youth soccer to date, this book covers all the bases in an engaging format. A handy reference long after you've read the book.

Go for the Goal: A Champion's Guide to Winning in Soccer and Life by Mia Hamm with Aaron Heifetz, 222 pages, $12.95, 1st Quill (2000)

For the fan who can't get enough of Hamm, the No. 1 female player in the world, this is the book. The narrative is in Hamm's voice and is packed with anecdotes about her career, her friendships, and playing tips for young players.

Make Your Move by Alfred Galustian and Charlie Cooke, 100 pages, $12.95, Lyons Press (2005)

Coerver Coaching, the world's number-one soccer skills teaching program, shows how to make 26 1v1 moves in step-by-step photos. It also presents exercises that youth coaches can use to teach the moves at practices.

The Peak Performance by Dr. Ronald W. Quinn, 104 pages, $17.45, QSM Consultants, P.O. Box 15176, Cincinnati, OH, 45215; 513–761–6240 (1990)

Quinn, the head coach of the Xavier University women's soccer team, presents sixty-one different soccer games for player development. Includes a number of sample practice planners. An important reference for every youth soccer coach.

Play-By-Play Soccer by Lori Coleman, 64 pages, $7.95, LernerSports (2000)

A book for eleven- to fourteen-year-olds who are new to the game or want to improve their skills. Includes lots of color photos and information on rules, positions, skills, tactics, and practice drills.

The Soccer Coaching Bible from the National Soccer Coaches Association of America (2004)

Top college coaches from across the U.S., including Anson Dorrance, Tony DiCicco, and Glen Myernick, offer insights on coaching priorities and principles.

Soccer for Dummies by Michael Lewis, 384 pages, $21.99, IDG Books Worldwide (2000)

A comprehensive book for every level of soccer fan. Covers a wide range of topics, from coaching to stretching to being a spectator of Major League Soccer.

Soccer for Juniors: A Guide for Players, Parents, and Coaches by Robert Pollock, 180 pages, $12.95, Macmillan (1999)

A very good book for soccer parents and parent-coaches. Pollock is a skilled writer and knows his subject matter. Includes in-depth explanations of basic skills, rules, and tactics.

Soccer Practice Games: 125 Games for Technique, Training and Tactics by Joe Luxbacher, $15.95, Human Kinetics (2003)

Luxbacher, author of several training guides, offers 125 games to use during youth practices to improve: warm-up and conditioning; passing and receiving; dribbling, shielding, and tackling; heading and shooting; tactical training; and goalkeeper training.

Videos and DVDs

The best sources for soccer videos and DVDs are Reedswain and Soccer Learning Systems. See the following "Catalogs" section.

All the Goals of the '99 Women's World Cup: All 123 goals of the 1999 Women's World Cup, seen from a number of angles. (53 minutes)

All the Right Moves: A collection of twenty moves are broken down in detail and shown in slow motion and at match speed. Then, watch pros use the moves in actual game footage. (35 minutes)

Champions of the World: Complete coverage of the exciting 1999 Women's World Cup, from the opening game to the U.S. penalty-kick victory over China in the final. (60 minutes)

Coaching Goalkeepers: Full of drills and exercises for ball handling, catching, diving, positioning, shot stopping, angles, throwing, kicking, foot skills, and more. (90 minutes)

FIFA Soccer Fever, The Definitive Guide to the World's Greatest Soccer Moments: A DVD produced to help celebrate FIFA's Centennial. Action from all 17 FIFA World Cups and all 4 FIFA Women's World Cups, as well as footage from FIFA's Youth and Futsal tournaments. (195 minutes)

How to Coach Young Soccer Players, Fun Games and Basic Skills: A good video for parents and novice coaches who want to keep soccer fun for very young players. (60 minutes)

The Master and His Method: Pelé, the greatest soccer player ever, presents a training program that includes ball control, passing, dribbling, trapping, physical conditioning, and more. (60 minutes)

A New Era: International stars and Coerver Coaching youth players from around the world demonstrate more than sixty games and drills in this three-video series; includes methods for individual and team development. (165 minutes)

NSCAA Soccer Tactics, On the Attack and Defending to Win: A two-disk DVD set from National Soccer Coaches Association of America. It features twelve tactical training sessions led by NSCAA National Staff Coaches. Each training session has approximately 20 minutes of instruction and also contains coaching cues. (240 minutes)

Really Bend It Like Beckham, David Beckham's Official Soccer Skills: A two-disk DVD set that uses slow motion to show off Beckham's genius, including space-making skills, turning skill, crossing, and closing down and defending. Also includes an interview and career highlights. (170 minutes)

Training Girls and Women to Win: Three-video series by April Heinrichs, the head coach of the U.S. Women's National Team. Technical, tactical, and psychological preparation geared toward the women's game. (215 minutes)

2002 World Cup Highlights: The most exciting plays of the most recent men's World Cup; includes great goals, spectacular saves, and more. (60 minutes)

Catalogs

Big Toe Sports
404 Holtzman Road
Madison, WI 53715
Orders: 800–444–0365
www.bigtoesports.com

> Large selection of footwear, authentic jerseys, balls, gloves, goals, referee gear, and more.

Eurosport
431 U.S. Highway 70A East
Hillsborough, NC 27278-9912
Orders: 800–934–3876
Customer Service: 800–487–7253
www.soccer.com

> Everything your club or team could possibly need: uniforms, balls, footwear, accessories, and more.

Reedswain
612 Pughtown Road
Spring City, PA 19475
Orders: 800–331–5191
www.reedswain.com

> Specializes in books, DVDs, and videos.

Soccer Learning Systems
P.O. Box 277
San Ramon, CA 94583
Orders: 800–762–2376
www.soccervideos.com

> Specializes in coaching videos, DVDs, and books.

Soccer Master
14188 Manchester Road
Manchester, MO 63011
Orders: 800–926–9287
www.soccermaster.com

Large selection of items for coaches, players, and teams.

Web Sites

www.fifa.com

The official Web site of the Fédération Internationale de Football Association, the international governing body of soccer. Includes a calendar of events, world rankings, and the complete Laws of the Game.

www.girlsoccerworld.com

A site for girls up to the age of eighteen who are interested in soccer as players, fans, referees, or coaches.

www.goal.com

In-depth coverage of soccer outside the United States. News about thousands of teams, players, and games abroad.

www.mlsnet.com

The official Web site of Major League Soccer. News, schedules, scores, stats, video highlights, ticket information, an "MLS for Kids" section, and more.

www.nays.org

The official Web site of the National Alliance for Youth Sports, an advocate for safe, positive, and fun youth sports.

www.saysoccer.org

The official Web site of the Soccer Association for Youth.

www.soccer.org

The official Web site of the American Youth Soccer Organization. Educational information for players, parents, coaches, referees, and instructors.

www.socceramerica.com

The official Web site of *Soccer America* magazine. Includes lots of up-to-date U.S. national-team and pro coverage. Also has helpful camp and tournament directories.

www.soccer-camps.com

Information on how to find a camp— or promote your camp if you're running one. Includes a state-by-state camp listing.

www.soccerhall.org

The official site of the National Soccer Hall of Fame and Museum. Includes features on the history of soccer and updates about programs and events at the Hall's campus in Oneonta, New York.

www.soccerinfo.com

The best Web site for college scores and schedules.

www.soccerpatch.com

A place for players to view, post, and trade patches and pins of their teams, towns, and tournaments.

www.soccertours.com

Comprehensive details on all levels of tours and tournaments from all over the world.

www.soccertv.com

"The ultimate guide to televised soccer" has detailed information on scheduled telecasts of upcoming games.

www.sportsparents.com

Need-to-know information for parents of young athletes: nutrition, psychology, injuries, sportsmanship, equipment, and more.

www.ussoccer.com

The official Web site of the U.S. Soccer Federation. Complete coverage of all the U.S. national teams, including ticket information.

www.ussoccerplayer.com

A site developed by U.S. national team players. It provides news, articles, games, puzzles, and playing and coaching tips.

www.womensoccer.com

Information about all aspects of the women's game. Immediate results, in-depth information, current news, TV listings, ticket information, and more.

www.youthsoccer.org

The official Web site of the U.S. Youth Soccer Association.

Glossary

Advantage Rule: The rule that allows the referee to decide to disregard a foul if stopping play would benefit the team that committed the foul.

Assist: The pass that leads to a goal.

Assistant Referees: Formerly called linesmen. Two subordinate officials in the single-referee format. Assistant referees indicate when a ball has gone out of bounds, indicate which team has possession, signal infractions and offsides, and consult with the referee in situations where the referee is not certain of what happened.

Bicycle Kick: An acrobatic overhead kick in which the player leaps into the air, with the legs moving as if pedaling a bicycle, and kicks the ball backward over his head. The bicycle kick isn't recommended for young players.

Box: See Penalty Area.

Cap: An appearance in an international match for one's country.

Chip: A high, lofted pass or shot over an opposing player.

Clear: To kick or head the ball away from the goal area to prevent the attacking team from scoring.

Cleats: Soccer shoes with studs on the bottom of the sole plate.

Corner Kick: An offensive free kick taken from the corner after the ball has been knocked over the goal line by a defender.

Cross: To pass the ball from one side of the field into the middle, usually in front of the goal.

Dangerous Play: Any play—such as raising the leg above waist height in order to kick the ball—that could cause injury to another player.

Defender: A player whose primary responsibility is to keep the other team from scoring.

Draw: A game that ends with the score tied.

Dribbling: Using the feet to move the ball along the ground.

Endlines: The boundaries on the ends of the field where each goal is located.

Far Post: The goalpost farthest from the ball.

Field: The playing area. Under international rules, the length (110–120 yards) of the field must be greater than the width (70–80 yards).

FIFA (Fédération Internationale de Football Association): The world governing body of soccer. FIFA, headquartered in Zurich, Switzerland, stages the World Cup and other major international tournaments.

Fifty-Fifty (50-50) Ball: A ball that is as near to a player of one team as it is to a player of the opposing team.

Flanks (Wings): The area of the field near the touchline, often used to describe defenders, midfielders, or forwards who play in that area.

Formation: The basic organization of the players at the start of a game, usually expressed by a series of three digits indicating the number of defenders, midfielders, and forwards. (Example: A 4-4-2 formation indicates a team is using four defenders, four midfielders, and two forwards.)

Forward (Striker): An attacking player whose primary responsibility is to score goals.

Foul (Infraction): An offense committed when a player breaks one of the rules of the game.

Free Kick: A kick taken to restart play after an infraction, a score, or the ball's going out of bounds over the endline. A direct free kick can result in a goal without requiring the ball to be touched by another player on either team. With an indirect free kick, the ball must first be touched by another player before a goal can be scored.

Goal: The 24-foot-wide-by-8-foot-high structure at each end of the field through which the ball must pass to score. A goal is scored when the entire ball crosses the goal line, between the goalposts and under the crossbar.

Goal Area: The 6-by-20-yard lined area in front of the goal where goal kicks are taken.

Goalkeeper (Keeper): The player who defends the goal, and the only player who may control the ball with any part of the hands or arms inside the penalty area.

Goal Kick: A kick taken by the defensive team after the ball is last played over the endline by the attacking team.

Golden Goal: A goal scored in sudden-death overtime that wins a game.

Half Volley: A kick taken just after the ball bounces.

Hand Ball: An infraction that is called when a player deliberately touches the ball with a hand or arm.

Hat Trick: Three goals scored in a game by one player.

Head: To clear, pass, or shoot the ball with the forehead.

Injury Time (Stoppage Time): The time—usually one to four minutes—the referee adds to the end of a half or a game to make up for time lost when the game was paused for injuries or other problems.

Instep: The top of the foot over the arch, used for kicking.

Marking: Closely guarding a specified opponent and being responsible for that player all over the field.

Match: A game.

Midfielder: A player whose primary responsibility is to move the ball from the defenders up to the forwards and to control the middle of the field. Midfielders have attacking and defending roles.

National Team: A team that represents a country in international competition.

Near Post: The goalpost closest to the ball.

Nutmeg: To dribble or shoot the ball between an opponent's legs.

ODP (Olympic Development Program): A program run by the U.S. Soccer Federation that identifies and trains high-level youth players in order to produce future national-team players.

Offside: An infraction called on an attacking player in the offensive half of the field if, at the moment the ball is played by a teammate, there are not at least two defenders between the player and the goal. Offside is only called when the player in the offside position is interfering with the play or gaining some advantage by being in that position.

Offside Trap: A defensive technique in which players move up quickly to catch their opponents in an offside position.

One-Touch: When a player receives a ball and passes or shoots it with the first touch, without trapping or dribbling it.

Overlap: To make a run past a teammate with the ball to create space for another pass or to distract defenders.

Own Goal: Accidentally kicking, heading, or deflecting a ball into one's own goal.

Penalty: A foul that results in the awarding of a penalty kick.

Penalty Area: The 18-by-44-yard lined area in front of the goal where the goalkeeper can touch the ball with his hands. Also referred to as the 18-yard box.

Penalty Kick (PK): A direct free kick taken from a spot 12 yards in front of the goal that occurs when an attacker is fouled in the penalty area.

Penalty Kick Shootout: A series of penalty kicks used to determine the winner after a game has ended in a tie. Five kicks are taken by each team, and the team that scores more goals wins. If the teams are tied after five kicks, the kicks continue until one team has scored more than the other after the same number of kicks.

Pitch: A British term for a soccer field.

Red Card: A card shown to a player by a referee to signal an ejection from the game. The player must leave the field and cannot be replaced. A player receiving a red card may face fines and further suspension.

Referee: The official in charge of the game: enforces the laws; official timekeeper; controls all substitutions; calls fouls and may caution or eject players; interprets rules; and makes sure ball and players' equipment conform to the rules.

Save: When the goalkeeper prevents the ball from going into the net.

Score: To make a goal, or the number of goals each team makes in a game.

Serve: To deliver an accurate pass to a teammate in a scoring position.

Shielding: Keeping yourself between the ball and the defender.

Slide Tackle: To leave your feet and slide on the ground in an attempt to win the ball or knock it away from an opponent.

Square Pass: A pass made to a player who is directly to the side of you.

Sweeper: The last player in the defense besides the goalkeeper; responsible for "sweeping" away all the balls that get past the rest of the team.

Tackle: To use one's feet and body to take the ball away from an opponent.

Throw-In: A method of putting the ball back into play after it has gone out of bounds over the touchline.

Touchlines (Sidelines): The boundaries on the two longer sides of a soccer field.

Trap: To bring the ball under control, usually with the foot, thigh, or chest.

Volley: A kick that is made while the ball is in the air.

Wall: Several players lined up to block a free kick that is taken close enough to the goal to be dangerous.

Wall Pass: Two players bypassing a defender by quickly passing to each other. The receiving player acts like a wall by letting the pass bounce off one foot, directing it into the path of the original passer, who is running behind the defender. Also referred to as a give-and-go pass or a one-two pass.

World Cup: The world championship of soccer; the international tournament featuring the best national teams in the world, held every four years.

Yellow Card: A card shown to a player by the referee to signal a caution for a flagrant infraction. A second yellow card results in the player's being ejected from the game.